STERLING BIOGRAPHIES

ROSA PARKS

Freedom Rider

Ruth Ashby

STERLING

New York / London
www.sterlingpublishing.com/kids

STERLING and the distinctive Sterling logo are registered trademarks of
Sterling Publishing Co., Inc.

Library of Congress Cataloging-in-Publication Data

Ashby, Ruth.
   Rosa Parks : freedom rider / Ruth Ashby.
      p. cm. — (Sterling biographies)
   Includes bibliographical references and index.
   ISBN-13: 978-1-4027-4865-3
   ISBN-10: 1-4027-4865-5
   1. Parks, Rosa, 1913–2005—Juvenile literature. 2. African American women—Alabama—
Montgomery—Biography—Juvenile literature. 3. African Americans—Alabama—Montgomery—
Biography—Juvenile literature. 4. Civil rights workers—Alabama—Montgomery—Biography—
Juvenile literature. 5. African Americans—Civil rights—Alabama—Montgomery—History—
20th century—Juvenile literature. 6. Segregation in transportation—Alabama—Montgomery—
History—20th century—Juvenile literature. 7. Montgomery (Ala.)—Race relations—Juvenile
literature. 8. Montgomery (Ala.)—Biography—Juvenile literature. I. Title.
   F334.M753P3718 2007
   323.092—dc22
   [B]
                                        2007019343

10 9 8 7 6 5 4 3 2 1

Published by Sterling Publishing Co., Inc.
387 Park Avenue South, New York, NY 10016
© 2008 by Ruth Ashby
Distributed in Canada by Sterling Publishing
c/o Canadian Manda Group, 165 Dufferin Street
Toronto, Ontario, Canada M6K 3H6
Distributed in the United Kingdom by GMC Distribution Services
Castle Place, 166 High Street, Lewes, East Sussex, England BN7 1XU
Distributed in Australia by Capricorn Link (Australia) Pty. Ltd.
P.O. Box 704, Windsor, NSW 2756, Australia
™ 2007 The Rosa and Raymond Parks Institute for Self-Development by CMG Worldwide, Inc.
www.RosaParks.org

Sterling ISBN-13: 978-1-4027-4865-3 (paperback)
      ISBN-10: 1-4027-4865-5

Sterling ISBN-13: 978-1-4027-5804-1 (hardcover)
      ISBN-10: 1-4027-5804-9

Designed by Josh Simons and Andrea Silenzi for Simonsays Design!
Image research by Susan Schader

For information about custom editions, special sales, premium and
corporate purchases, please contact Sterling Special Sales
Department at 800-805-5489 or specialsales@sterlingpub.com.

Contents

Events in the Life of Rosa Parks

1913

February 4, 1913
Rosa Louise McCauley is born to James McCauley and Leona Edwards McCauley in Tuskegee, Alabama.

1918
Rosa begins school in a one-room schoolhouse in Pine Level, Alabama.

1925
Rosa enrolls at Miss White's Industrial School for Girls in Montgomery, Alabama.

1929
Rosa drops out of school to care for her sick grandmother, Rose Edwards.

March 25, 1931
Nine young black men, known as the Scottsboro Boys, are arrested and charged with raping a whit woman. Raymond Parks becomes involved in their defense.

December 1932
Rosa marries Raymond Parks in Leona McCauley's home in Pine Level.

1934
Rosa Parks earns her high school diploma when she is twenty years old.

1941
Parks is hired at the newly integrated Maxwell Air Force Base.

December 1943
Parks joins the NAACP and becomes a volunteer secretary.

April 1945
Parks passes the required literacy test and registers to vote.

May 17, 1954
The Supreme Court hands down the *Brown v. B* *of Education* decision, declaring "separate but equal" facilities in schools to be unconstitution

July 1955
Parks attends the Highlander Folk School in Monteagle, Tennessee, to take workshops on how to implement desegregation.

August 28, 1955
Emmett Till is beaten and killed in Mississippi. His death shocks America and helps galvanize the civil rights movement.

December 1, 1955
Parks is arrested after refusing to give up her seat on a bus to a white person.

December 5, 1955
Black citizens of Montgomery begin a bus boycott to challenge existing bus segregation laws.

November 13, 1956
The U.S. Supreme Court rules that bus segregation is unconstitutional.

January 7, 1956
Parks loses her job at the Montgomery Fair department store.

Summer 1957
The Parks family moves to Detroit, Michigan.

December 21, 1956
The Montgomery Bus Boycott ends after 381 days. The Montgomery buses are integrated.

August 28, 1963
Parks attends the March on Washington rally, where Dr. Martin Luther King, Jr., gives his famous "I have a dream" speech.

July 2, 1964
President Lyndon B. Johnson signs the Civil Rights Act.

March 1, 1965
Parks begins working in the Detroit office of Congressman John Conyers.

March 25–26, 1965
Parks attends the Selma to Montgomery march in favor of voting rights.

April 4, 1968
Dr. Martin Luther King, Jr., is assassinated in Memphis, Tennessee.

1979
Parks's mother, Leona McCauley, dies at age 9

1987
Parks founds the Rosa and Raymond Parks Institute for Self-Development to teach young people about the history of civil rights in America.

1992
Parks publishes her first book, *My Story*, an autobiography for young people.

September 9, 1996
Parks receives the Presidential Medal of Freedom from President Bill Clinton.

2000
The Rosa Parks Library and Museum is opened by Troy University in Montgomery.

October 24, 2005
Rosa Parks dies at age 92 at her home in Detro

2005

One Courageous Act

*Before King there was Rosa Parks. She is who
inspired us . . . to be fearless when facing our
oppressors.*

—Nelson Mandela

As a plane circled the landing strip at Detroit's Metro
Airport, seventy-seven-year-old Rosa Parks waited for a
first glimpse of her hero, South African Nelson Mandela.
The seventy-one-year-old Mandela had spent twenty-seven
years in prison for resisting the **apartheid** policies of the
all-white South African government. Now, he had come
to the United States to meet the president, but he also
wanted to meet Rosa Parks.

As Mandela walked down the stairs, he spotted the
small, gray-haired woman and made his way over to her,
"Rosa Parks! Rosa Parks!" he began to chant, and the
crowd of thousands began to chant along: "Ro-sa Parks!"

"You sustained me while I was in prison all those
years," Mandela told Parks, giving her a big hug. Rosa
Parks, after all, inspired freedom fighters everywhere.

Nearly fifty years early, she had performed a
courageous act that had set into motion the whole modern
civil rights movement in America. Her story and the
Montgomery Bus **Boycott** of 1955 proved that one person
could indeed make a difference. Quiet, determined, and
fearless, Rosa Parks fought back against racism and
oppression and changed the course of history.

CHAPTER 1

Down Home in Alabama

By the time I was six, I was old enough to realize that we were actually not free.

Rosa Parks grew up in the Deep South at the beginning of the twentieth century, in a place so segregated that African Americans could not eat, study, worship, or travel alongside whites. Although slavery had been abolished more than fifty years earlier, black people still had not gained equality under the law or in everyday life. Even as a child, Rosa knew that her friends and family were not included in America's pledge of "liberty and justice for all." Someday she would help to change that.

Tuskegee, Alabama, where Rosa Louise McCauley was born on February 4, 1913, embodied her people's hope for a better future. It was home to the Tuskegee Institute, a renowned industrial college for black students founded by educator Booker T. Washington. He believed that every African American should have an education and the opportunity to excel.

Tuskegee, Alabama, where Rosa Louise McCauley was born on February 4, 1913, embodied her people's hope for a better future.

A Heritage of Black and White

Rosa's mother, Leona McCauley, trusted wholeheartedly in education, too. She took to heart Washington's belief that all people could achieve a better life through hard work and thrift. The granddaughter of slaves, Leona had grown up with stories about what life was like before the Civil War and emancipation. Leona's maternal grandfather, James Percival, was actually a white man who arrived from Scotland as an indentured servant. In order to pay back the cost of the boat fare to America, he bound himself to work for a white farmer in Pine Level, Alabama, for a number of years. Percival ended up marrying another member of the household, a black slave with whom he had nine children. The couple bought land in Pine Level after the Civil War ended.

Rosa's mother, Leona McCauley, trusted wholeheartedly in education, too.

Leona had a mixed-race heritage on her father's side, too. Sylvester Edwards, Leona's father, was the son of a white plantation owner and his black housekeeper, who both died when he was quite young. The friendless boy was abused by the whites on the plantation. Rosa recounted later that the overseer would beat her grandfather and "tried to starve him, wouldn't let him have any shoes." As a result, Edwards grew up with a "very intense, passionate hatred for white people." Rosa added that it was Sylvester Edwards, her grandfather, who taught her not to "put up with bad treatment from anybody."

Perhaps due to his painful childhood, the last thing Edwards wanted was for any of his children to work as maids or farm hands for rich white folks. He encouraged Leona to obtain an education so she could support herself, and she attended all-black Payne University in Selma, Alabama. Although she did

Booker T. Washington (1856–1915)

Booker T. Washington was the most prominent African American of the early twentieth century. Born into slavery in Virginia in 1856, he worked as a youth in a coal mine before becoming a houseboy for a sympathetic white woman who encouraged him to get an education. At age sixteen, Washington enrolled in the Hampton Institute in Hampton, Virginia, where his fierce work ethic so impressed school officials that they recommended him for a series of teaching jobs.

Booker T. Washington, shown in this c. 1903 photograph, was an influential educator and spokesman for the African American community.

It was his appointment as principal of the new Tuskegee Normal and Industrial Institute in 1881 that gave Washington a national platform as spokesperson for his race. In this post–**Reconstruction** era, Washington preached self-reliance and hard work. In his famous 1895 Atlanta Compromise speech, he told his black fellow citizens to "Cast down your bucket where you are" and to earn respect through manual labor. "There is as much dignity in tilling the field," he proclaimed, "as in writing a poem."

His compromise on **segregation** led the more radical black reformer W.E.B. DuBois to label Washington scornfully as "The Great Accommodator." Yet Washington devoted his life to promoting the "commercial, agricultural, educational, and industrial advancement" of his race, and his relationships with prominent white politicians and businessmen helped to raise millions of dollars for African American education. His 1901 autobiography, *Up From Slavery*, proved an inspiration to millions.

not complete her undergraduate degree, she did earn enough credits to become a teacher. She was teaching in a one-room schoolhouse in Pine Level when she met a handsome carpenter named James McCauley and married him in April 1912.

They moved to Tuskegee, where Leona gave birth to their first child, Rosa Louise. Leona had bright plans for her family's future. She wanted James to get a job teaching carpentry at Tuskegee Institute so that they could live in faculty housing and Rosa could benefit from the best education possible. James, however, had other ideas. He preferred life on the road, picking up construction jobs wherever he could and then moving on. The family left Tuskegee and wandered, living for a while with James's family in Abbeville, Alabama. James and Leona continued to disagree, and eventually Leona, Rosa, and her little brother Sylvester returned to Pine Level to live with Grandmother and Grandfather Edwards. Rosa saw her father little after that.

The Tuskegee Normal and Industrial Institute was a school that was originally established to train African Americans in practical trade skills. This 1902 photograph shows hard-working students in one of its workshops.

Leona found a teaching job in a town eight miles away. Each Monday, Leona's father would hitch up his mule and drive her to Spring Hill in an old wagon. At the end of the week, he would pick her up again and bring her home. Meanwhile, Rosa and her little brother remained with her grandparents on their farm. She missed her mother, of course, but farm life had its compensations.

A Country Girl

The eighteen-acre Edwards farm, inherited from Rosa's great-grandfather James Percival, supported cows, chickens, and a variety of fruit and nut trees. Rosa picked walnuts, peaches, apples, and pecans to make pies and jams. On hot summer days, she would grab her rod and reel and go fishing for bass and crawfish in the nearby creek. She was proud of her talent for putting the worm on the hook without feeling squeamish.

Rosa and her family ate off the land—hearty food such as possum, rabbit, squash, and black-eyed peas—and never went hungry. Actual money, though, was scarce. Her mother used her teaching income to buy necessary items like cloth at the country store so that she could sew clothes for her children. Sometimes Rosa and little Sylvester would sell eggs and chickens for extra cash.

Rosa and her family ate off the land—hearty food such as possum, rabbit, squash, and black-eyed peas—and never went hungry.

The family also made ends meet by laboring on the local cotton plantation. Every fall from the time she was six years old, Rosa worked as a field hand. In the spring she would prepare the ground for planting, and would chop and pull weeds from around the base of the new cotton plants. Then in the fall she would pick the cotton. Even small children, she remembered, worked from "can" to "can't"—from sunrise, when you could see well enough to work, to sunset, when you could not. "I never will forget how the sun just burned into me," she recalled. "The hot sand burned our feet whether or not we had our old work shoes on." Any child who pricked a finger on the sharp cotton bolls and bloodied the cotton was beaten by the overseer.

Like Rosa and her brother Sylvester, many black children labored in the cotton fields of the South from dawn to dusk, as shown in this 1899 stereograph.

Because fieldwork was available only in the growing season, Rosa and her brother attended school just five or six months a year, from late fall to early spring. Like other black children in Pine Level, she attended a one-room schoolhouse on the grounds of the local African Methodist Episcopal (AME) church. One woman was in charge of teaching fifty or sixty children the basics of "readin', writin', and 'rithmetic." Rosa, who picked out her first words when she was three or four, "thought it was great to be able to take a book and sit down and read." She especially enjoyed fairy tales. At recess, she played traditional ring games like Rise Sally Rise and Ring Around the Rosie.

This crowded, one-room, black-only school in Georgia in 1941 was heated by the potbellied stove in the center, just like Rosa's school in Alabama.

Lessons in Racism

School gave Rosa one of her first lessons in racism. Her old, all-black school was made of wood, with wooden shutters instead of glass in the windows. The local white school, on the other hand, was brick, with real plate-glass windows. The white students' school was heated during the winter, but if black students wanted a warm school they had to bring their own logs to burn in the iron stove. In addition, black children had to walk to their school, while white children took school buses to theirs. Rosa thought the inequality was particularly unfair because the new segregated white school, including the buses, was paid for by taxes from both white and black citizens. Sometimes, as she and her friends were trudging to school, children on passing buses would actually pelt them with garbage.

Rosa grew up hearing stories about slavery and knew how badly Grandfather Sylvester had been treated when he was a boy.

Even though he was part white, Sylvester despised whites so much that he refused to let Rosa and her brother play with the white children on the plantation. "He was always doing or saying something that would embarrass or agitate white people," Rosa recalled. Because he was light-skinned, he liked to fool white people into thinking he was white himself. "Name's Martin," he'd say, shaking a strange white man's hand. "Glad to meet you, Mr. Martin," the man would respond. Later, when the unsuspecting white man discovered Martin was really black, he would be humiliated. In the early decades of the twentieth century, the average white man in the South would always call a black man by his first, not his last, name, and he would never, ever shake his hand.

The year 1919 was a time of turmoil for black people in the South. **World War I** had just ended, and African American soldiers coming back from Europe were proud of their service

Soldiers in the 369th Negro Regiment stand proudly at attention in this World War I photograph.

overseas and eager to assert their rights in their home states. Alarmed, white racists were just as determined to keep blacks "in their place." All summer, members of the white hate organization, the Ku Klux Klan, rampaged through Alabama, burning black homes, churches, and businesses and terrorizing their black neighbors. At night, Rosa's grandfather would sit in his rocking chair by the door, waiting to defend his house in case of attack. Seven-year-old Rosa, scared yet unwilling to miss anything, would sleep on the floor by his side. "I remember thinking that whatever happened, I wanted to see it," she wrote later. "I wanted to see him shoot that gun." The masked terrorists never did come to Rosa's house. However, that summer, black people across the South were beaten and **lynched**.

Just like her grandfather, Rosa stood up to "bad treatment." Once when she was about ten years old, a white boy named Franklin threatened Rosa with his clenched fists and said he would punch her. Rosa, in turn, threatened to throw a brick at him, and Franklin backed off. Upon hearing of the incident, her grandmother scolded her. "You'll be lynched before you're twenty years old," she warned.

Unlike her grandfather, Rosa did not grow up hating white people. She remembered various acts of kindness. Once a white soldier from the North patted her on the head and told her she was a cute little girl. Rosa's family told the story again and again, marveling at his kindly nature. Years later, Rosa remembered a nice white woman in town who would take her fishing for bass. Rosa remained open-minded. She knew that all white people weren't bad.

CHAPTER 2

Welcome to Montgomery

We were taught to be ambitious and to believe that we could do what we wanted in life.

For years Leona scrimped and saved every extra penny she earned, hoping that her daughter would get the higher education that she herself had never completed. When the little school in Pine Level closed down for lack of money, Rosa and Sylvester walked to nearby Spring Hill, where their mother taught in a church school. Rosa remembered that her mother was a "good teacher" who taught girls "sewing, crocheting, knitting, and needleworking" in addition to the usual academic subjects. When Rosa completed sixth grade, Leona sent her to Alabama's capital city, Montgomery, to live with relatives and to further her education.

Life in Montgomery

In 1924, Montgomery proudly referred to itself as "the cradle of the Confederacy." The first capital of the Confederate States of America during the Civil War, it still boasted a statue of Confederate President Jefferson Davis in front of the gleaming white capitol building. Following the Civil War and the era of Reconstruction, Montgomery became a bustling port city crisscrossed by streets full of streetcars, mule-drawn wagons, and automobiles and lined with fashionable modern stores. Montgomery even had a small but prosperous black community, composed

Revival of the Ku Klux Klan

America's most notorious terrorist organization, the Ku Klux Klan, was founded after the Civil War by former Confederate soldiers. Enraged by the defeat of the South, Klansmen began to attack freed black men and white Northerners who came South during Reconstruction. Klansmen disguised themselves in white hoods and robes to intimidate, beat up, and murder anyone who tried to give blacks their rights. In the 1870s, the Republican Congress passed laws to clamp down on the Klan, and it was essentially destroyed.

It was a movie that gave birth to the new Klan in 1915. D. W. Griffith's *Birth of a Nation* romanticized the white-robed defender of white womanhood, and new chapters of the Klan grew up from the North to the South. This new organization, though, was

The white hoods and burning crosses of the Ku Klux Klan, seen in this c. 1965 photograph, were calculated to strike fear into the hearts of observers.

not just anti-black but also was anti-immigrant, **anti-Semitic**, and anti-Catholic. In hundreds of communities throughout the North and the South, ghostly figures in white hoods held huge rallies with burning crosses, then rode through black neighborhoods and terrorized the residents. Renewed racism after World War I helped swell the organization's ranks. By 1924, the Klan reached its all-time peak of about four million members, and then gradually lost widespread popularity. In the 1960s, the Klan was responsible for numerous house and church bombings and for the murders of civil rights supporters.

Montgomery was the first capital of the Confederacy and is the home of the Alabama State Capitol building shown here.

of doctors, business owners, professors, and other professionals. Many worshipped at the city's center of black middle-class life, the Dexter Avenue Baptist Church.

However, even for eleven-year-old Rosa, the exciting sights and sounds of Montgomery could not disguise a harsh truth. Like many other southern cities, Montgomery was part of the Jim Crow South. Jim Crow was a system of laws and traditions that kept blacks and whites separated. By law, blacks and whites drank from separate drinking fountains, attended different schools and churches, rode in separate railroad cars, ate in separate restaurants, and were buried in separate cemeteries.

Even though these laws may have appeared unconstitutional, they were upheld by the **Supreme Court** decision of *Plessy v. Ferguson*, in 1896, which stated that a system of "separate but equal" facilities was indeed constitutional.

In Montgomery's streetcars, blacks had to sit in the far rear of the cars. In 1900, black leaders had actually led a boycott of the streetcars to protest such discrimination. The streetcar companies lost so much money that they gave in, and for a short time, blacks and whites sat side by side in the cars. Renewed racism after the First World War had ended even such token **integration**. Jim Crow was firmly in place by the time Rosa came to the city. When she heard about the 1900 boycott, she was "saddened to think how we had taken one foot forward and two steps back."

Jim Crow laws kept blacks and whites segregated. A black man enters the "colored entrance" of a movie house in Belzoni, Mississippi, 1939.

Reconstruction and After

The eleven states of the former Confederacy were in political and economic chaos after the Civil War. During the period known as Reconstruction, the Republican Congress tried to impose order and ensure that African Americans got their rights. In December 1865, the Thirteenth Amendment, which prohibited slavery, was ratified by the states. The Fourteenth Amendment (1868) granted African Americans their citizenship and "equal protection of the laws"; the Fifteenth Amendment (1870) gave black men the right to vote. Freedmen took advantage of their new rights by voting black leaders into state and federal office, including two to the U.S. Senate and fifteen to the House of Representatives.

Reconstruction officially ended in 1877 when U.S. troops left the South. With them went the hope of black citizens for equal citizenship. All-white state legislatures quickly passed a series of measures to separate the races and guarantee white supremacy. This system of racial segregation was known as "Jim Crow," after a handicapped, servile black character from a 1830s **minstrel show**. It lasted throughout the South for the next seventy-five years.

An 1867 engraving shows newly freed black citizens in Washington, D.C., casting their votes under the watchful eyes of both whites and blacks. African Americans in the South lost their right to vote when Reconstruction ended in 1877.

Because of Jim Crow laws, blacks in many states were forced to use separate accommodations, like this black man who is drinking from the "colored" fountain in a streetcar terminal in Oklahoma City, Oklahoma, 1939.

The formal segregation surprised Rosa. She was used to whites making blacks feel inferior. However, Pine Level was so tiny that it had no drinking fountains, trains, or streetcars. Blacks naturally kept to themselves. When Rosa first saw drinking fountain signs reading "For Whites Only" or "For Colored," she wondered whether the water tasted or looked different. Finally, she discovered that the water "had the same color and taste. The difference was who got to drink it from which public fountain."

Plessy v. Ferguson

In 1892, a New Orleans shoemaker named Homer Plessy challenged the Jim Crow laws in Louisiana. Knowing that he was breaking the law, he sat down in a white-only car on a segregated train and was arrested. After being found guilty, he appealed his case all the way to the Supreme Court. The majority of the justices, however, found that separating the races in public did not violate the equality of the two races under the law. "If one race be socially inferior to another," the decision read, the "Constitution of the United States cannot put them upon the same plane." In other words, separate-but-equal facilities for the two races was constitutional.

The May 18, 1896, Supreme Court ruling in *Plessy v. Ferguson* upheld a Louisiana state law that allowed for "equal but separate accommodations for the white and colored races."

Only one judge, Justice John Harlan, dissented. "Our Constitution is color-blind," he declared, "and neither knows nor tolerates classes among citizens. In respect of civil rights, all citizens are equal before the law." Unfortunately, the doctrine of "separate but equal" became the law of the land for fifty years. Not until 1954 did another Supreme Court case, *Brown v. the Board of Education of Topeka, Kansas*, strike down *Plessy v. Ferguson*.

Rather than stand in the rear of a segregated streetcar, Rosa preferred to walk to school every day from her aunt's home across town. Her path took her through a white neighborhood. One day, a white boy zipping by on roller skates tried to shove her off the sidewalk. Rosa turned right around and pushed him back. His mother took one look at this aggressive black girl and threatened to put her in jail. Rosa defended herself by pointing out that the boy had pushed her first and that she did not like being pushed.

When Rosa's mother heard about the incident, she promptly moved Rosa into the home of another relative who lived in an area where Rosa would no longer have to walk through a white neighborhood. Leona knew that her seemingly quiet daughter could get into trouble just by asserting her rights. "Nobody ever bossed Rosa around and got away with it," a school friend remembered.

Miss White's School

Even though Rosa had to live under such racial pressures, it was worth being in Montgomery just so she could attend the legendary Montgomery Industrial School for Girls, better known as Miss White's.

Alice L. White, a white **abolitionist** teacher from Massachusetts, had founded the school in 1866 to give freed black girls the chance of an education. There were still no public high schools for black students in Montgomery in the 1920s. Miss White and the other white northern teachers were despised by the surrounding white community, which refused to have anything to do with them. Years earlier, the school had even been burned down by a white mob, only to be rebuilt. In 1924, it was an imposing three-story brick building, which was a school to three hundred eager students.

This 1899 photograph shows a sewing class in Augusta, Georgia. Education for black girls traditionally stressed practical skills as well as academic subjects.

At Miss White's, Rosa studied academic subjects such as English, geography, science, and mathematics. She also learned "domestic science," which included sewing, cooking, and other homemaking skills. She learned basic nursing skills, too, because white hospitals in the South did not accept black patients, and Rosa and her classmates would someday be responsible for nursing their families at home. All in all, the girls received a practical vocational education that emphasized, as a classmate remembered, that "cleanliness was next to godliness."

The most important virtue Miss White taught Rosa, though, could not be learned from the pages of a book. It was self-respect. "I . . . learned that I should not set my sights lower than anybody just because I was black," Rosa said. "We were taught to be ambitious and to believe that we could do what we wanted in life." Years later, many of Rosa McCauley's fellow students took the discipline and self-confidence they had learned at Miss White's and put it into practice during the civil rights movement.

The most important virtue Miss White taught Rosa, though, could not be learned from the pages of a book. It was self-respect.

While Rosa was in Montgomery, her life improved in another way, too. Since early childhood, Rosa had suffered from nearly constant colds and sore throats and missed far too much school. She had great difficulty swallowing—probably due to enlarged tonsils—and was very small for her age. Before she started at Miss White's, her mother brought her to a Montgomery infirmary to have her tonsils removed. It took Rosa a long time to become completely well, but afterward, she shot up to a normal height.

By 1928, Miss White was a very old, frail woman. The constant harassment by the white community had finally taken its toll, and she closed her school after sixty-two years and moved back to the North. Luckily, a junior high for black students had just opened up in Montgomery, and Rosa was able to attend Booker T. Washington Junior High through ninth grade. Then, because there was still no black public high school in the area, she went to the laboratory school at Alabama State Teachers' College for Negroes.

There, student teachers earned credit for teaching high-school-level courses as they worked toward their degrees. Rosa stood out as a "self-sufficient, competent, and dignified" girl, classmate Mary Fair Burks recalled, "who did not seek to outshine anyone in the classroom but was always prepared." Burks added that Rosa never disobeyed the rule that girls always wear a clean uniform and stockings. "Her teachers regarded her as a model student."

"Her teachers regarded her as a model student."

Earning a high school diploma had been one of Rosa's dreams. However, when she was sixteen, her grandmother fell ill and Rosa dutifully returned to Pine Level to help nurse her. Her grandmother died a month later, but then Leona McCauley fell ill, too, and Rosa dropped out of school. She accepted the responsibility of caring for her mother and the farm without complaint. "It was something that had to be done," she felt.

It was while she was living at home that Rosa Parks met the man she would marry.

CHAPTER 3

Finding a Cause

With the vote would come economic improvements. We would have a voice.

At first, it seemed an unlikely match. Eighteen-year-old Rosa McCauley wasn't even attracted to twenty-eight-year-old Raymond Parks when a friend introduced them. She later admitted that she had never liked light-skinned men (except her Grandfather Sylvester), and she thought the Montgomery barber was "too white." Parks, however, certainly liked Rosa. He drove to her mother's house several times before she agreed to accompany him on the first of many Sunday rides in his sporting red automobile. During their long country drives, he told her his life story.

Courtship and Marriage

Raymond Parks was born on February 12, 1903, in Wedowee, Alabama. His white father left while he was still a baby, and he was raised by his black mother, Geri Culbertson Parks, who taught him to read and write. As a black boy in an all-white neighborhood, he wasn't allowed to attend the local white school. After his mother died while he was in his teens, he became sexton (groundskeeper) for a white Baptist church before moving to Tuskegee to become a barber. In 1931, when he met Rosa, he had moved to Montgomery and was working at O. L. Campbell's barbershop.

Rosa was impressed by this kind young man who talked so knowledgeably and intelligently. "I was very impressed by the fact that he didn't seem to have that meek attitude—what we called an '**Uncle Tom**' attitude—toward white people," she remarked later. With Raymond, Rosa could talk freely about problems of racial discrimination. It didn't take her long to discover that he was a genuine civil rights activist—the first she had ever known. He was widely read in the works of contemporary black writers such as W.E.B. DuBois and Langston Hughes, who were featured in such prominent black newspapers as *The Crisis* and the *New York Amsterdam News*.

Smitten, Raymond asked Rosa to marry him on their second date, but she took longer to make up her mind. They were finally wed in December 1932 in her mother's house in Pine Level, surrounded by family and friends. With Raymond's encouragement, Rosa completed her high school degree at the laboratory school.

She was one of the few black people in Montgomery with a high school diploma. "In 1940, seven years after I got my diploma, only seven out of every hundred had as much as a high school education," she later pointed out. Even with the degree, she could find only menial work as a seamstress and hospital aide. The United States was in

Langston Hughes, who wrote poetry, stories, and plays about the black experience, is one of the best-beloved African American poets.

As the Great Depression worsened, millions of Americans lost their homes and jobs. Here, unemployed men in Washington, D.C., line up at a soup kitchen in 1936 for free food.

the **Great Depression** in the 1930s, and few jobs were open to anyone. In her twenties, Rosa had no opportunity to pursue whatever ambitions she might have had. Instead, she gradually became involved in the cause that would consume the rest of her life: the fight for civil rights.

The Scottsboro Boys

Raymond Parks was one of the first members of the Montgomery chapter of the National Association for the Advancement of Colored People (NAACP). The organization was devoted to pursuing justice for blacks throughout the country. During the 1930s, Raymond was obsessed by one of the most controversial scandals of the decade: the case of the Scottsboro Boys. These were nine black teenagers, ranging in age from thirteen to nineteen, who were riding the rails from Tennessee to Alabama on March 25, 1931, and became involved in an argument with two white drifters, known as "hobos." The hobos flung gravel at the boys and the boys hurled it back. At the next station, the whites got off the train and demanded the arrest of the black boys. Two prostitutes who were also thrown off the train joined in, claiming that the boys had raped them. As a result, all nine boys were arrested on charges of rape and thrown in jail.

When the case went to trial in Scottsboro, Alabama, the all-white jury convicted eight of the boys of rape and sentenced them to death. Quickly, Parks and other members of the NAACP scrambled to organize a legal defense fund called the National Committee to Defend the Scottsboro Boys.

Danger All Around

The work of the National Committee to Defend the Scottsboro Boys was so dangerous that Raymond discouraged Rosa from attending any of the meetings, which were held in nearby homes. Rosa was proud of her husband, though. "He could have been beaten or killed for what he was doing," she remarked. "Later I came to understand that he was always interested in and willing to work for things that would improve life for his race, his family, and himself."

For fear of the police, one man with a gun would stand lookout at the meetings. Once when the meetings were held at the Parkses' house, "The whole table was covered with guns," Rosa remembered. She was so frightened that she went out onto the back porch, possibly to distance herself from all those firearms. It depressed her to think that nothing had changed since the days long ago when she had waited with her grandfather for the Ku Klux Klan to attack.

For fear of the police, one man with a gun would stand lookout at the meetings.

The NAACP

By the turn of the twentieth century, African Americans were trapped in a deadly web of segregation and discrimination. In 1908, a brutal anti-black riot in Springfield, Illinois, resulted in a meeting of concerned individuals in New York City. More than forty prominent black and white leaders, including black activist W.E.B. Dubois, anti-lynching crusader Ida B. Wells-Barnett, and Jewish social worker Henry Moscowitz, formed an organization dedicated to fighting for the rights of minorities, including African Americans, Native Americans, and Asian Americans.

The organization was called the National Association for the Advancement of Colored People (NAACP), and it chose to battle segregation through the courts. Gradually the NAACP became an influential organization, with its membership growing from 9,000 in 1916 to 90,000 in 1920, to 500,000 in the 1940s.

Over decades, in numerous court cases, the NAACP Legal Defense and Education Fund challenged the "separate but equal" doctrine established by the Supreme Court's *Plessy v. Ferguson* ruling. Their campaign culminated with the Court's *Brown v. Board of Education* case in 1954, which disputed segregation in public education.

Active recruitment of African Americans helped NAACP membership soar between its founding and the 1940s, when this photograph was taken.

The nine imprisoned Scottsboro Boys confer with their attorney in 1933.

Another time, when Rosa was sitting on the front porch swing, two policemen on motorcycles roared up and down the street. The day before, two of Raymond's NAACP colleagues had been killed by the police, and now he was late coming home from a meeting. The police so intimidated Rosa that her nervous shaking caused the whole swing to tremble. Luckily, they never stopped at the house. When Raymond finally did come home, he snuck in the back door so the policemen wouldn't see him.

In 1932, the U.S. Supreme Court overturned the Scottsboro conviction, and the case was thrown back to Alabama for a second trial. This time, doctors for the defense proved that the prostitutes had lied about the rape. Nevertheless, in the final compromise deal struck in 1937, only four of the boys were freed, while the other young blacks were given long prison sentences.

"The whole Scottsboro ordeal was a travesty of justice," Rosa declared bitterly. "It's a monument to America at its worst." Not until 1950 was the last defendant released on parole.

A First Glimpse of Integration

If the Scottsboro case helped educate Rosa to the realities of racial inequality; so did being hired as a secretary at the Maxwell Field Air Force Base in 1941. At the start of **World War II**, President Franklin Roosevelt desegregated military bases across the United States. Being on an integrated base was a revelation for Rosa. For the first time, she ate in a cafeteria and traveled on trolley cars next to white people. When she had to get back on a segregated trolley car to return to Montgomery, she felt humiliated. "You might just say Maxwell opened my eyes up," she commented later. "It was an alternative reality to the ugly racial policies of Jim Crow."

Rosa Parks knew that the leaders of the NAACP had been responsible for persuading President Roosevelt to desegregate the bases. Although the NAACP stood on the front line in the legal fight for racial justice and equality, Raymond Parks dropped out of the NAACP in 1943. He didn't feel that the educated professionals who ran the organization had enough respect for working-class men like him.

Working for the NAACP

However, that same year, Rosa decided to join the NAACP herself. She went to her first meeting hoping to catch a glimpse of an old friend from Miss White's school named Johnnie Mae Carr. Her friend, though, wasn't there that evening. As Rosa was

However, that same year, Rosa decided to join the NAACP herself.

the only woman present, she was promptly made secretary. Too "timid to say no," as she recalled, she immediately took out a pad and began to take notes.

For the next twelve years, Rosa Parks was the volunteer secretary of the Montgomery chapter of the NAACP. She was one of the few women involved in the civil rights movement in the 1930s and 40s and worked for Edgar Daniel (E. D.) Nixon, an NAACP organizer who became president of the chapter. As a sleeping-car porter on the railroad, Nixon had traveled the country and seen racial integration in the North. It inspired him to go back to Montgomery and work toward fair employment

Black men wearing tuxedos protest segregation by staging a mock funeral for Jim Crow laws in 1944.

and welfare for blacks. Although Rosa Parks described Nixon as a "proud, dignified man who carried himself straight as an arrow," he was somewhat of a traditionalist—once remarking "women don't need to be nowhere but in the kitchen."

"What about me?" Rosa challenged him. Laughing, Nixon admitted that she was a very good secretary.

Rosa spent countless hours working in Nixon's home office, typing notes, writing letters, and organizing meetings. The NAACP was a national central office for spreading information about racial injustice, and Rosa was responsible for keeping records of crimes targeting blacks and of court cases. Information about horrific brutality—rapes, beatings, and lynchings—crossed her desk. Rosa helped publicize these cases and organize legal defenses for black people who had been unjustly accused of crimes themselves. Much of her time was also spent working on two Jim Crow issues: voting rights and the desegregation of Montgomery buses.

Testing Voter Registration

When Rosa Parks investigated voter registration, she discovered that only thirty-one people in Montgomery's black population of 50,000 were registered—and that some of them were dead. She decided to test the system by trying to register to vote herself. The hurdles, she knew, would be high and numerous in order to discourage black citizens from even trying to register. First, the registration office was only open at certain hours—usually when most people were working—and those hours were not

When Rosa Parks investigated voter registration, she discovered that only thirty-one people in Montgomery's black population of 50,000 were registered.

Voting Rights

It took a lot of effort to **disenfranchise** African Americans. In 1870, the Fifteenth Amendment to the Constitution gave blacks the right to vote: "The rights of the citizens of the United States to vote shall not be denied or abridged . . . on account of race, color, or previous condition of servitude." That year, as many as one million freedmen registered to vote, and black candidates were elected to state and national office.

Yet after Reconstruction ended in 1877, the Confederacy passed laws to restore white supremacy. Voters had to pay poll taxes, pass literacy tests, and own property. In some cases, so-called "grandfather clauses" stated that only citizens and their descendants who had voted before 1867 retained the right to vote. Naturally, no black men had voted before 1867—that was the year the Fourteenth Amendment had granted them citizenship! All these laws were applied disproportionately to African Americans. Nearly all black citizens in the South were disenfranchised by 1910.

An 1874 cartoon by Thomas Nast states that anti-black persecution after the Civil War was even "worse than slavery."

announced ahead of time. Second, she would have to take a so-called literacy, or reading, test, which was generally given to blacks but not to whites. This test was not really an assessment of whether she could read. It was a long, complicated questionnaire testing her

A long line of black citizens wait patiently outside a Baptist Church to register to vote.

detailed knowledge of the Constitution. Few could pass it.

Parks was resolute. "From the start the NAACP, to me at least, was about empowerment through the ballot box," Parks recalled. "With the vote would come economic improvements. We would have a voice." The first time she took the test, she never received the certificate in the mail and was told she didn't pass. The second time, she was denied again. Yet she thought she answered all the questions correctly. So the third time she tried, in 1945, she secretly copied her answers on a separate sheet. That way, she could challenge the registration board if necessary. But lo and behold, her registration arrived in the mail on time, and Rosa rejoiced.

Only one last obstacle remained. She had to pay her poll tax. According to Alabama law, all voters had to pay $1.50 a year to vote, starting when they were twenty-one years old. For Parks, now thirty-two, payment would include all the years from the time she became twenty-one. She owed $16.50, which was a lot of money in 1945. Still, she paid—and on the next Election day, Rosa Parks cast her vote for the first time in the race for Alabama's next governor.

CHAPTER 4

Separate but Not Yet Equal

It was painful to get on a bus and have to pass by all those empty seats up front in order to stand in the rear.

In 1945, World War II ended, and American troops started to come home. Among them was Rosa's brother, Sylvester McCauley, who had been a medic in both the European and Pacific war regions. In Europe, black soldiers were treated like liberators who had helped with the war, just like their white counterparts.

McCauley returned to Alabama and his wife and children, expecting to be welcomed as a war hero. Instead, like other black men in uniform, he was mocked and threatened by local white racists, who tried to hammer home the point that there was no such thing as equality and justice for the black man in the South. McCauley, who had risked his life for his country, couldn't even register to vote. In disgust, he announced he was leaving Alabama—and within the year, moved his family to Detroit, Michigan.

Staying Put in Montgomery

Sylvester begged Rosa and Raymond to leave, too. So Rosa, for the first time in her life, traveled north to visit her brother. She marveled at the integrated bus system and the freedom to eat in restaurants and go to shows and museums. However, she was appalled by the story of the ugly Detroit race riot of 1943, when a racially motivated

The Great Migration

When Sylvester McCauley moved to Detroit after World War II, he joined a "great migration" of African Americans from the South to the North. The movement began around 1910, when rural blacks began to move to northern cities in search of jobs, and continued until the 1950s. Millions of African Americans moved to cities such as New York City; Chicago, Illinois; Detroit, Michigan; St. Louis, Missouri; and Los Angeles, California.

During World War I, black workers took over northern jobs vacated by white immigrant workers who had joined the armed forces. In addition, a beetle infestation ruined cotton crops and forced **sharecroppers** out of the fields and onto the road north. During World War II, President Franklin Roosevelt integrated all war-related industries, and black workers found jobs in northern factories. By 1960, about ninety percent of all blacks in the North lived in urban areas.

During and after World War II, black workers traveled north to take advantage of new manufacturing jobs. This 1942 photo shows an integrated work force building a plane on a factory assembly line.

A white mob pushes over a car owned by a black man during the Detroit, Michigan, race riots of 1943.

beating sparked a series of riots that killed thirty-four people—both white and black—and injured thousands. Rosa concluded that "racism was almost as widespread in Detroit as in Montgomery." Besides, Raymond had no intention of leaving Alabama, so they "put aside any ideas of moving to a northern promised land that wasn't."

Instead, Rosa continued to work at the NAACP, doing field research, issuing press releases, and keeping the books. One of her most rewarding experiences was being adviser to the NAACP Youth Council. She and Raymond had never had children, and she loved being around young people. As E. D. Nixon noted, "Kids just love[d] Mrs. Parks to death. They had a special bond, an understanding that was very rare indeed, full of hugs and all that." Parks encouraged the young high school activists to try to integrate Montgomery's main public library, which did not allow

Rosa Parks led a chapter of the NAACP Youth Council much like this group in Charlotte, North Carolina, 1942.

black people to take out books. Yet no matter how many times the students requested books from the librarians, they were always turned away.

Bus Segregation in the South

The local Jim Crow law that the NAACP was most determined to abolish had to do with bus segregation. The rules governing Montgomery's buses were complicated and treacherous. Of the thirty-six seats, the front ten were reserved for whites. The back ten were reserved for blacks, unless, of course, there were no more seats for white passengers. The middle sixteen were first-come, first-serve—at least in theory.

Of course, any white person could seize any black person's seat whenever he or she wanted. If a white person sat down in a particular row, all the blacks in that row had to stand up and move, too, to avoid any physical contact between the races.

"Buses weren't something optional, like restaurants," explained Fred Gray, a black Montgomery lawyer. "Every day, the bus situation put the issue of what it meant to be black squarely before you."

Of course, any white person could seize any black person's seat whenever he or she wanted.

Racist bus drivers could make the experience even worse. Sometimes after black customers paid their fare at the front of the bus, drivers (all of whom were white) would make them exit the bus and enter again through the rear door. At other times, when the customer got off the bus to re-enter in the back, the driver would simply drive away. Riding the buses in Montgomery was an everyday humiliation for Rosa Parks. "The question of where we had to sit on the bus wasn't a little thing," she once explained. "It was painful to get on a bus and have to pass by all those empty seats up front in order to stand in the rear." Most painful, she felt, was the way little black children were made to feel inferior every time they had to move to the back of the bus.

Confrontation on the Bus

One afternoon in 1943, Parks had a run-in with one of the meanest drivers in town. After boarding the Cleveland Avenue bus and paying her fare, she started to move toward the back, noticing that it was so crowded with black passengers that some were standing in the rear step well. The driver, though, demanded that she exit the bus and get on again through the rear door. Firmly, she replied that she was "already on the bus and didn't see the need of getting off and getting back on."

"If you don't get on through the back door, just get off and stay off," the driver snapped.

When Parks just stood there, the driver grabbed her coat sleeve and pulled her forward. She held her head high and did not struggle. Then, when they reached the front, she "accidentally" dropped her purse and sat down in one of the empty white seats while she picked it up.

The driver was furious that she had managed to sit in one of the forbidden seats. "Get off my bus!" he roared.

"I will get off," she said calmly. "You better not hit me."

She exited with dignity. Parks didn't want to ever meet that bus driver again. So from then on, she avoided getting on any bus that James Blake was driving—at least for the next twelve years.

Jim Crow laws in many parts of the country segregated black and white Americans in public transportation. A c. 1955 sign on a Los Angeles bus instructs black customers to sit from the very last seat forward.

A Landmark Case

Sometimes it seemed as though legal discrimination would never end. However, a landmark Supreme Court case in 1954 gave Parks and her friends new hope.

For decades, the NAACP had been looking for the perfect case to challenge *Plessy v. Ferguson*, which made "separate but equal" the law of the land. They found it when a Topeka, Kansas, father decided to challenge the law that forbade his seven-year-old daughter Linda from going to the new all-white elementary school a few blocks from home. Instead, she had to make the long trip across the railroad tracks to a "colored" school.

Oliver Brown, the plaintiff in *Brown v. Board of Education*, poses with his wife, Leola, and his daughters, Linda (left) and Terry, in front of their house in Topeka, Kansas, 1953.

In 1951, Oliver Brown and eleven other black families sued the Topeka school district—and lost their case in the local federal court. The judge ruled that only the Supreme Court had the authority to overturn the separate-but-equal **precedent** established by *Plessy*.

Rosa, who knew all about segregated schools from her own childhood, followed the case closely. She remembered the old wooden schoolhouse with the wood-burning stove. She also remembered her mother being paid less than white teachers for the same work.

Brown v. Board of Education

Seventeen states, encompassing 11,173 school districts, had segregated public schools when the NAACP argued the *Brown v. Board of Education* case before the Supreme Court. Facilities for black students were usually poor and rundown and far inferior to those for whites. The NAACP actually combined five different cases under *Brown*, involving school districts from South Carolina, Delaware, and Virginia in addition to Kansas.

In a sweeping decision, the Court concluded that not only were segregated schools unconstitutional, but that such separation harmed black children greatly. Chief Justice Earl Warren, writing for the unanimous opinion in the case, stated that: "To separate [black children] from others of similar age and qualifications solely because of their race generates a feeling of inferiority as to their status in the community that may affect their hearts and minds in a way unlikely ever to be undone . . . We conclude, unanimously, that in the field of public education the doctrine of 'separate but equal' has no place. Separate educational facilities are inherently unequal."

Chief Justice Earl Warren led the Court that declared "separate but equal" facilities for black citizens were unconstitutional.

The NAACP presented the case to the U.S. Supreme Court in December 1952. The Court deliberated for a year and a half before reaching a decision. Chief Justice Earl Warren wanted to make sure that such an important decision had the support of all the justices. On May 17, 1954, in a unanimous ruling, the Supreme Court pronounced that separate but equal was not constitutional—and never could be.

Finally, the federal government had come down on the side of civil rights for African Americans. Although the decision didn't actually order the immediate desegregation of southern schools, the principle of mandatory integration had been established. If segregated schools were against the law, then so were segregated restaurants, drinking fountains—and buses. At least, that was what African Americans hoped. "You can't imagine the rejoicing among black people, and some white people, when the Supreme Court decision came down," Parks recounted in her autobiography. "It was a very hopeful time." Four days after the decision, an African American English professor at Alabama State University named Jo Ann Robinson launched the first fight against Montgomery's segregated buses.

Finally, the federal government had come down on the side of civil rights for African Americans.

Trying to Challenge the Bus System

Robinson had been determined to do something about the bus service since 1949, when, as a newcomer to the Montgomery bus system, she had inadvertently sat down in a "white" seat and was ordered off the bus by the furious driver. "I tumbled off the bus and started walking back to the college," she wrote in her memoir *The Montgomery Bus Boycott and the*

Women Who Started It. "Tears blinded my vision; waves of humiliation inundated me; and I thanked God that none of my students was on that bus to witness the tragic experience. I could have died from embarrassment."

Robinson never rode a Montgomery bus again. Instead, she took her complaint back to the Women's Political Council (WPC), an activist organization committed to challenging segregation, and told them what had happened. When she became WPC president a few years later, she made plans for a general boycott of the buses. On May 21, 1954, she even sent a letter to the Montgomery mayor W. A. "Tacky" Gayle threatening the city with a boycott if the system did not change. Gayle ignored the warning.

All that Robinson and the women of the WPC needed now was a rallying cause. They found one in Claudette Colvin, a feisty fifteen-year-old at Booker T. Washington High School. On March 2, 1955, she boarded a bus determined to take a stand. After she sat down in the middle of the bus, a white person got on and the driver ordered her to move. Staring straight ahead, Colvin sat tight. The driver summoned two policemen, but still Colvin would not budge. "I do not have to get up," she declared as they hauled her out of her seat. "It's my constitutional right to sit here just as much as that [white lady]. It's my constitutional right!" When Colvin fought back, the police handcuffed and booked her.

> *"I do not have to get up," she declared as they hauled her out of her seat. "It's my constitutional right to sit here . . ."*

The black community was electrified by news of Colvin's defiance. Finally, thought E. D. Nixon of the NAACP and Jo Ann

Robinson, they had a winnable court case. They petitioned the bus company, asking that it hire more black bus drivers and treat black customers with more respect. Rosa Parks, though, refused to sign the petition. She didn't want to be

They petitioned the bus company, asking that it hire more black bus drivers and treat black customers with more respect.

humiliated when white people refused to grant their request. "I had decided that I would not go anywhere with a piece of paper in my hand asking white folks for any favors."

However, as local NAACP secretary, Parks did accompany Nixon and Robinson to jail to ask Colvin whether she would be willing to be the **plaintiff** in a **class action** desegregation suit. The young girl had just agreed when Nixon caught wind of a rumor that Colvin was pregnant—and the case was promptly dropped. The NAACP did not want to risk the possibility that the media or general public would disapprove because it was representing an unwed mother. In a class action suit, the plaintiff represents many people. Any plaintiff would receive a lot of publicity and might even be subject to threats and intimidation. Nixon felt (and Parks agreed) that the ideal plaintiff had to be not only strong and determined but also morally above reproach.

The boycott would have to wait until they had a perfect plaintiff.

CHAPTER 5

A Renewed Spirit

I was forty-two years old, and it was one of the few times in my life up to that point when I did not feel any hostility from white people.

Even while volunteering for the NAACP, Rosa continued to earn a living. In the early 1950s, she was doing tailoring at Sol Crittenden's tailor shop, where she earned about twenty-five dollars per week. She and her family barely managed to scrape by on this small amount of money. Later, she switched to the tailoring shop at the Montgomery Fair department store.

By this time, Rosa was helping to support both her ailing mother, who had moved in with her, and her husband. Raymond Parks also suffered from ill health and made little money barbering, so Rosa had to take in extra sewing and housework on the side. In 1954, E. D. Nixon introduced her to a new client, the socialite Virginia Durr. Through this remarkable woman, Rosa Parks would be offered an extraordinary opportunity.

A New Friend

Virginia Foster Durr was a southern woman who broke all the rules. She was raised in Birmingham, Alabama, to be a genteel southern lady. Yet she chose to go to college—unusual for a southern woman at the time—and she decided to go north to Wellesley College in

Massachusetts. There she was assigned to a dining table with a black student. Going against her upbringing, Virginia, who had been taught never to treat a black person as an equal, promptly sat down at the same table.

Virginia later married progressive Birmingham lawyer Clifford Durr, who was employed by Franklin D. Roosevelt's administration in the 1930s and 1940s. She, meanwhile, worked with the black educator Mary McLeod Bethune and other black and white liberals to abolish the poll tax and Jim Crow segregation. By the 1950s, the Durrs' activities in Washington, D.C., led their adversaries to label them as **radicals**. They decided to leave the capital to open a law practice in Montgomery. They returned to

Educator Mary McCleod Bethune worked in Franklin D. Roosevelt's administration to promote equal opportunities for black Americans. Here she chats with students at Bethune-Cookman College, which she founded in Dayton Beach, Florida.

Alabama knowing that if they tried to fight segregation, they would be spurned by white society. Nevertheless, Clifford served his mostly black clients, and Virginia was welcomed by Jo Ann Robinson and the Women's Political Council. She became friends with E. D. Nixon and joined an interracial prayer group that included Rosa Parks.

> *"[Rosa is] thoroughly good and brave, and the people here have the highest respect for her."*

Rosa talked to Virginia by the hour about discrimination and civil rights strategies. Durr was impressed by the "very quiet, determined, brave," demeanor of her new friend. She "is not at all sophisticated and [is] very churchgoing and orthodox in most of her thinking," Durr said of Rosa. "But thoroughly good and brave, and the people here have the highest respect for her. When she feels at ease and gets relaxed, she can show a delightful sense of humor, but it is not often." Though Rosa became close to the older woman, she hesitated to call Virginia by her first name, even when invited to. So for more than twenty years, Rosa and Virginia knew each other as Mrs. Parks and Mrs. Durr.

The Highlander School

Durr understood Parks's fervent interest in the cause of civil rights. Just a few months after the *Brown* decision, she recommended Parks for a ten-day training workshop at the Highlander Folk School in Monteagle, Tennessee, to discuss how to carry out the Supreme Court's ruling to integrate the public schools. The Highlander, founded by white activist Myles Horton in 1932, trained people on how to fight for workers' rights and racial equality. The school attracted participants from all over the country, both black and white. Over the years, some of those

Myles Horton, founder of the Highlander Folk School, fought for racial equality years before the civil rights movement gained national attention.

who came to Highlander were black civil rights leaders, including Martin Luther King, Jr., and Julian Bond. Horton said in a TV interview that "At Highlander, anywhere you went everybody was equal. I always said we were too small and too poor to discriminate."

It was also a little known fact that the most famous anthem of the civil rights movement, "We Shall Overcome," actually came from the Highlander Folk School.

Rosa decided to go because, as she told Virginia Durr, she wanted things to be better for the young people she worked with at the NAACP. As for herself, she said sadly, she felt "she had been destroyed long ago." In July 1955, she took a leave of absence from her job in the tailoring department of Montgomery Fair department store. Armed with a small scholarship and Virginia Durr's suitcase, Rosa Parks took a bus to Chattanooga,

"We Shall Overcome"

Originally a gospel song written by minister Charles Tindley in about 1900, the song was discovered by Highlander co-founder Zilphia Horton, who taught it to folk musician Pete Seeger. He added some verses and taught it to others, who reintroduced it to Highlander. Black and white participants would hold hands to sing the song, which became the inspiration to civil rights groups across the country.

> We shall overcome,
> We shall overcome
> We shall overcome some day
> Oh, deep in my heart
> I do believe
> We shall overcome some day.

Civil rights leaders band together to sing "We Shall Overcome."

Tennessee. From there, a white man picked her up and drove her the rest of the way to the two-hundred-acre school. She arrived tense and nervous and was upset about ongoing racial discrimination. Gradually, however, she calmed down enough to enjoy herself.

Highlander was a revelation to Parks. For the first time in her life, she lived on an equal basis with whites. "We forgot about what color anybody was," she recalled. "I was forty-two years old, and it was one of the few times in my life up to that point when I did not feel any hostility from white people." Because the school was so small and poor, all participants shared chores like cleaning and cooking. Daily assignments were posted on a bulletin board. One of Parks's greatest joys, she admitted, was "enjoying the smell of bacon frying and coffee brewing and knowing that white folks were doing the preparing instead of me."

Each day, Rosa Parks attended workshops on voting rights and desegregation.

Learning at the Highlander

Each day, Rosa Parks attended workshops on voting rights and desegregation. One of her teachers was Septima Clark, a former South Carolina teacher who was fired from her job for joining the NAACP. At Highlander, she ran the citizenship school that prepared black people to take the literacy test and obtain their voter registration. For Parks, the fifty-seven-year-old Clark served as a role model. She hoped that some of Clark's "great courage and dignity and wisdom" would rub off on her.

Clark could feel the depths of anger beneath Rosa's quiet, polite exterior. "Rosa Parks was afraid for white people to know she was as militant as she was," Clark remembered later. "She

At the Highlander Folk School, Rosa Parks attended workshops, like the one seen in this photograph, on civil rights issues along with fellow activists Myles Horton and Septima Clark. Rosa Parks is circled.

didn't want to speak before the whites that she met up there, because she was afraid they would take it back to the whites in Montgomery." Gradually, though, the warmth and camaraderie wore away Parks's reserve. She relaxed enough to join in some of the recreational activities, such as sing-alongs and swimming.

Rosa also shared her experiences of discrimination with a sympathetic audience. "Myles Horton just washed away and melted a lot of my hostility and prejudice and feelings of bitterness toward white people, because he had such a wonderful sense of humor," Parks admitted. "I found myself laughing when I hadn't been able to laugh for a long time."

When the workshop ended, Horton asked all attendees for a written assessment. How could they apply the activist strategies they had learned at Highlander to combating inequality in their hometowns? Parks was pessimistic about the chances for change in Montgomery. "Nothing would happen there," she said, "because blacks wouldn't stick together." It was her experience that Montgomery's blacks were too used to being subservient to whites to confront them in an organized way. On a personal level, though, she was far more hopeful. Highlander, she said, had given her "strength to persevere in [her] work for freedom."

How could they apply the activist strategies they had learned at Highlander to combating inequality in their hometowns?

CHAPTER 6

Tired of Giving In

I was not old, although some people have an image of me as being old then. I was forty-two. No, the only tired I was, was tired of giving in.

Rosa Parks returned from the heaven of Highlander to the hell of the sweltering basement in Montgomery Fair department store, where she had to be "smiling and polite no matter how rudely you were treated." After the equality of Highlander, she found it more and more difficult to face the segregated buses. As often as possible, she walked.

Events also continued to heat up that summer and fall of 1955. Shortly after her return from Highlander, Rosa Parks and the nation were shocked by a particularly vicious example of white brutality that occurred in Mississippi. It surrounded the horrific torture and killing of a fourteen-year-old boy named Emmett Till by two white men, who were found not guilty by an all-white jury. Rosa and hundreds of thousands of people in America and around the world saw the grisly picture of Emmett's battered head in magazines and newspapers. This incident outraged black America and brought civil rights issues to the forefront.

Work at the NAACP

On August 14, 1955, Parks met a man whose name would soon ring across the land. At an NAACP meeting held at the Metropolitan United Methodist Church, she sat

The Emmett Till Case

Emmett Till was a young man from Chicago, Illinois, who was visiting relatives in Mississippi and was not familiar with the social norms of the South. While in a local shop, he made some innocent remarks to a white woman. Four days later the woman's husband and at least one other man kidnapped Emmett, and then tortured and beat him. Finally, they shot Till in the head and dumped his mangled body in the Tallahachie River.

When his body was discovered a few days later, Till's mother insisted on bringing her son's body back to Chicago for a public funeral, where the grizzly pictures of the young man were taken and published.

Emmett Till and his mother, Mamie Till Bradley, in Chicago, before his fatal trip to Mississippi.

Although the two men accused of Till's death—Roy Bryant and J. W. Milam—went on trial, they were acquitted by an all-white jury. However, in October 1955, they agreed to tell southern journalist William Bradford Huie the true story of that horrendous night in exchange for $4,000. Although Huie knew the two men were immune from further persecution—under U.S. law, no one can be tried for the same crime twice—he wanted to let the "facts indict the community. It will shake people in Mississippi."

Forty-nine years later, the U.S. Justice Department decided to reopen the Till case, to ascertain whether anyone else was involved in the murder. By that time, both Milam and Bryant were dead. They had indeed gotten away with murder.

NAACP executive director Roy Wilkins (left), Dr. Martin Luther King, Jr., (center), and civil rights organizer A. Philip Randolph (right) shared a common dream: political and social equality for African Americans.

transfixed as she listened to the brilliant young preacher Martin Luther King, Jr., speak about the *Brown* decision. King had recently been named as the minister of Montgomery's most influential black church, Dexter Avenue Baptist. Her friend Johnnie Mae Carr nudged her in the ribs and whispered, "He's something else."

"I was very impressed by his eloquence," Parks recalled. "He looked like he might have been a student in college instead of a minister at a very prestigious church." Parks immediately sent King a formal invitation to the next meeting of the NAACP

Executive Committee. Clearly a new black leader had arrived in town, and Parks wanted to enlist him in Montgomery's most important civil rights organization.

Fall 1955 was a busy time for Rosa Parks. Besides working full-time at Montgomery Fair, she also organized NAACP events. In September, she met dynamic New York Congressman Adam Clayton Powell, Jr., who was in Alabama to discuss desegregation strategies with other activists. Rosa took notes while Powell and E. D. Nixon discussed plans of action. "He [Powell] was very funny and forceful in his approach," Rosa remembered. "And he always called me 'honey.'"

In October, another black woman, eighteen-year-old Mary Louise Smith, refused to give up her seat on a Montgomery bus and was arrested for disobeying the segregation laws. Although Smith was already sitting in the "colored" section, the bus driver asked her to move for a white woman who had no seat. The

Rosa met and worked with civil rights leaders E. D. Nixon (center) and Congressman Adam Clayton Powell (right). The two activists are shown here at a civil rights rally in New York City in 1956.

NAACP considered making her their star plaintiff in a court case, then changed its mind. Smith, Nixon decided, had family problems and was not the model plaintiff they were looking for. They wanted someone who would be above criticism when exposed to national media attention.

A Fateful Day

On December 1, 1955, Rosa Parks left work shortly after 5:00 p.m. and walked down to Court Square to get the Cleveland Avenue bus home. The Christmas lights were already twinkling, but Parks's mind was on other things. She was planning an NAACP workshop for young people at Alabama State College in a few days and was trying to persuade the president of the college to let her have a classroom. She was also sending out mailings for the upcoming NAACP elections.

When the lime-green-and-gold bus came to a stop, Parks absentmindedly got on and paid her fare without even looking at the bus driver. Not until she sat down in a seat in the first row of the "colored" seats did she notice that he was James Blake—the belligerent bus driver who had ordered her off his bus years before. Next to her sat a black man looking out the window; two black women chatted across the aisle.

At the next stop, more white people got on and nearly filled up the "whites only" section. One more stop, and those seats were filled; one man remained standing. James Blake swiveled around and ordered, "Move, y'all, I want those two seats." The four people in Rosa's row stared at him silently. "Y'all better make it light on yourselves and let me have those seats!" Blake barked.

Slowly the two men and one woman stood up and moved toward the back. Parks moved her legs to let the man pass. Then, rather than standing up herself, she slid over to the window and

The Cleveland Avenue city bus that Rosa Parks boarded on December 1, 1955, is displayed in the Henry Ford Museum in Dearborn, Michigan.

looked out. "I did not see how standing up was going to 'make it light' for me," she said later. "The more we gave in and complied, the worse they treated us."

The bus fell silent. Rosa thought about her childhood, about her grandfather waiting for the Klan with a shotgun across his lap. Remembering the indignities and fear her family had suffered over the years, she suddenly felt as if she had the "strength of her ancestors with her."

Remembering the indignities and fear her family had suffered over the years, she suddenly felt as if she had the "strength of her ancestors with her."

Blake got up and loomed over her. "Are you going to stand up?" he barked.

"No," Rosa said quietly.

"Well," I'm going to have you arrested."

She looked straight at him. "You may do that."

Arrested!

Rosa Parks waited. She had made her decision. Now others would make theirs.

Blake was flustered, but he knew what he should do. Following regulations, he radioed his supervisor for directions. "Did you warn her, Jim?" the supervisor asked him. Blake replied that he had. "Well, then, Jim, you got to exercise your power and put her off, hear?"

Blake got off the bus to call the police. Inside, one rider remembered, it was totally silent. "It was like a mosque. . . . You could have heard a pin drop. It was as if we were all praying to Allah." In small groups, people began to get off. Some asked for transfers to another bus. Obviously the one they were on would not be moving anytime soon.

Blake got off the bus to call the police. Inside, one rider remembered it was totally silent.

A few minutes later, a police car pulled up and two policemen clambered up the stairwell. Officer F. B. Day asked Parks why she didn't move when she was asked to.

"Why do you all push us around?" Parks answered quietly.

Day shrugged. "I don't know, but the law is the law and you're under arrest."

With that, he picked up her purse; Officer D. W. Mixon grabbed her shopping bags, and together they escorted Parks to the squad car. Thankfully, they were neither rough nor abusive. On their way to the police desk at City Hall, Day again asked her why she didn't stand up when the driver told her to. Parks, her mind far away, did not answer him.

The police report on the arrest of Rosa Parks read, in part: ". . . the bus operator said he had a colored female sitting in the white section of the bus, and would not move back."

Jailed

At the station, Parks was booked and fingerprinted. Thirsty after her ordeal, she requested a drink of water from the water fountain.

"Go ahead," Day said.

Officer Mixon interrupted. "No, you can't drink no water," he snapped. "It's for whites only. You have to wait until you get to the jail."

Please, she asked, could she make a phone call? Again, the answer was a firm no.

The matron led her down the dark, dank jail corridor and put her in her cell. The door clanged loudly—and Rosa Parks was behind bars.

The door clanged loudly—and Rosa Parks was behind bars.

One of the women in the cell gave Parks a cool drink of water from her metal cup. Rosa listened as the woman chatted about her own predicament. She told Parks that she had been in jail two months for threatening her abusive boyfriend with an ax. Now, the boyfriend was ready to kiss and make up, but the woman didn't want to have anything to do with him. Unfortunately, no one else knew the woman had been imprisoned, and she had no money to raise bail herself. The poor woman also couldn't reach her brothers.

Rosa promised that when she got out of jail, she would call the woman's brothers for her. As the woman reached for a piece of paper on which to write down her brothers' phone numbers, the matron reappeared and ordered Rosa to follow her. Down the dark corridor, they came to a pay phone. Finally, Rosa would be allowed to call home.

Leona McCauley answered the phone. "I'm in jail," Parks told her mother. She explained what had happened. "See if Parks will come down here and get me out."

"Did they beat you?" her frantic mother wanted to know.

No, they hadn't, Rosa told her. Her husband and mother, both upset about the arrest, were relieved that no one had touched her.

"I'll be right there," Raymond reassured his wife. She knew it might take a while, because they did not own a car. However, a friend came by a few minutes later after hearing about Rosa's arrest, and Raymond jumped into the friend's car to rescue his wife.

Bailed Out of Jail

Word had indeed already spread throughout the community. Another passenger on the bus had informed Bertha Butler, a friend of Mrs. E. D. Nixon, who notified her husband. Nixon immediately called the jail to find out the charges against Rosa, but the police officers wouldn't talk to a black man. Nixon then asked his friend Clifford Durr to call the jail instead. Durr found out that Rosa had disobeyed the segregation laws and that bail was set at one hundred dollars.

The Parkses had very little money, and the Durrs were practically broke, so Nixon offered to pay the fee. Then, he, Clifford, and Virginia Durr drove to the jail to get Rosa. On the way over, they discussed the possibility of turning this into the NAACP case for the Supreme Court.

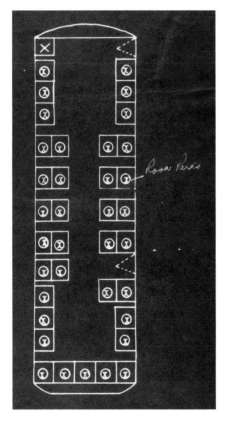

This layout, which shows where Rosa Parks sat on the Cleveland Avenue bus on December 1, 1955, is part of the court records.

Rosa Parks had barely gotten back to the jail cell when word came of her release. The matron rushed Parks out so fast that her cell mate didn't have the chance to hand Parks the piece of paper on which she'd written down the phone numbers. She threw it out of the cell, and it landed at Parks's feet. Rosa picked it up and stuffed it in her pocket.

Rosa Parks had barely gotten back to the jail cell when word came of her release.

The first person Parks laid eyes on was Virginia Durr. Years later, Durr remembered that it "was a terrible sight to see: this gentle, lovely, sweet woman, whom I knew and was fond of, being brought down by a matron. She wasn't in handcuffs, but they had to unlock two or three doors that grated loudly." Virginia threw her arms around Rosa and hugged her, Rosa remembered, "as if we were sisters."

E. D. Nixon posted bail, and they collected Rosa's purse and bags. The trial date was set for Monday, December 5. Just as they were leaving, Raymond Parks sped up in his friend's car. He raced into the jail and enveloped Rosa in a big hug. Then, two and a half hours after Rosa Parks entered the jail, she was free to leave. She didn't realize until after it was over, she wrote later, just how upset she was.

Afterward, some said that Parks had remained seated because her feet were so tired. Again and again, she set the record straight. "People always say that I didn't give up my seat because I was tired, but that isn't true. I was not tired physically, or no more tired than I usually was at the end of a working day," she explained. "I was not old, although some people have an image of me as being old then. I was forty-two. No, the only tired I was, was tired of giving in."

CHAPTER 7

Start of the Civil Rights Movement

More important, never before had the black community of Montgomery united in protest against segregation on the buses.

In two cars, they returned to the apartment on Cleveland Avenue, where her mother was waiting. By then it was after nine o'clock at night, and Rosa wanted to eat, relax, and eventually, fall into bed. However, everyone was agitated by what had happened and stayed up late talking. Finally, E. D. Nixon asked Parks the all-important question: Would she be willing to be the plaintiff in a class-action suit to challenge Montgomery's Jim Crow laws?

Rosa's answer was cautious. First, she told Nixon, she would have to discuss the matter with her husband and mother. Sure enough, Raymond Parks was horrified at the idea. "Oh, Rosa, don't do it!" he cried out. "The white folks will kill you!"

Rosa knew that his concern was well founded. If she became the public face of the desegregation movement, she and Raymond ran the risk of being harassed by **white supremacists**. She would probably lose her job, and Parks himself might be arrested on some made-up charge. Also, she was worried about the strain of the publicity on her mother, who was elderly and already in poor health.

The Perfect Plaintiff

Yet Rosa Parks knew where her duty lay. Although she hated being the center of attention, she would do whatever it took to change the soul-destroying system of segregation with which she had grown up. "I was determined to achieve the total freedom that our history lessons taught us we were entitled to," Parks explained later, "no matter what the sacrifice." Yes, she told Nixon, she would do it.

E. D. Nixon was jubilant. "My God, look what segregation has put in my hands!" Finally, he had found his perfect plaintiff.

Rosa understood why he was so pleased. "I had no police record," she explained in her autobiography. "I'd worked all my life. . . . The white people couldn't point to me and say that there was anything I had done to deserve such treatment except to be born black."

The first step would be for Rosa Parks to challenge the bus segregation laws on the grounds that they were unconstitutional. She hoped that her lawyer would be Fred Gray, one of two black attorneys in Montgomery and a close friend of both Nixon and Parks. The group knew that it would cost money to take the case all the way to the Supreme Court, money that none of them had. In order to raise the money, they would have to enlist the help of the national NAACP Legal Defense and Education Fund and its head, lawyer Thurgood Marshall. They knew Marshall would support them.

That much decided, the guests left, and Rosa fell into bed. While she tried to sleep, others stayed up, making plans to change the world.

Thurgood Marshall (1908–1993)

In 1930, Thurgood Marshall was denied entrance to the University of Maryland Law School because he was black. Three years later, after graduating first in his class from Howard University Law School, he was hired by the NAACP Legal Defense Fund to argue civil rights cases. His first battle was to sue the University of Maryland to admit another African American student, Donald Gaines Murray. His victory in that case was the first of many anti-segregation triumphs for Marshall. He headed the team that argued *Brown v. Board of Education* and went on to win many battles against discrimination in education, housing, and jobs. In 1967, President Lyndon Johnson appointed Marshall a justice of the Supreme Court. As the first black member of the Court, he continued to interpret the Constitution as a living document that continually needed analysis to ensure true equality of opportunity for all Americans. "The true miracle of the Constitution," Marshall once declared, "was not the birth of the Constitution, but its life."

A champion of equal rights, Thurgood Marshall was the first African American appointed to the Supreme Court.

Mobilizing the Community

Late Thursday night, December 1, E. D. Nixon started a chain of phone calls that would mobilize Montgomery's black community to action. The first person he called was Fred Gray, the lawyer whom he hoped would oversee Rosa's case. Sure enough, Fred agreed immediately and phoned the Parkses' home to offer his services for free.

Attorney Fred Gray, only 24 when he represented Rosa Parks in her court case, also became Martin Luther King, Jr.'s first civil rights lawyer.

Next, Gray called Jo Ann Robinson, head of the Women's Political Council. As Robinson recounts in her memoir, it was already 11:30 p.m. when the phone rang. "Fred was shocked by the news of Mrs. Parks's arrest," she wrote. "I informed him that I already was thinking that the WPC should distribute thousands of notices calling for all bus riders to stay off the buses on Monday, the day of Mrs. Parks's trial. 'Are you ready?' he asked." Without hesitation, Robinson assured him that the WPC was.

Robinson realized that she had no time to lose. She would not wait to receive Rosa's permission to order a boycott of the city buses on Monday. If the black community was to be notified, she would have to do it the next day, while schools were in session and businesses were open. Friday was now only minutes away. Quickly Robinson drafted an announcement, and then called a friend in the business department at Alabama State College and made arrangements to meet him in his office. At midnight, she, her friend, and two students met in the mimeograph room in the administration building and ran off thousands of handbills,

The Bus Boycott Announcement

Jo Ann Robinson wrote, typed, and duplicated a historic notice after she heard about Rosa Parks's arrest. By the next afternoon, she had distributed tens of thousands of leaflets. These are the words that black Montgomery read on December 2, 1955:

This is for Monday, December 5, 1955

Another Negro woman has been arrested and thrown in jail because she refused to get up out of her seat on the bus for a white person to sit down.

It is the second time since the Claudette Colvin case that a Negro woman has been arrested for the same thing. This has to be stopped.

Negroes have rights, too, for if Negroes did not ride the buses, they could not operate. Three-fourths of the riders are Negroes, yet we are arrested, or have to stand over empty seats. If we do not do something to stop these arrests, they will continue. The next time it may be you, or your daughter, or mother.

This woman's case will come up Monday. We are, therefore, asking every Negro to stay off the buses Monday in protest of the arrest and trial. Don't ride the buses to work, to town, to school, or anywhere on Monday.

You can afford to stay out of school for one day if you have no other way to go except by bus.

You can also afford to stay out of town for one day. If you work, take a cab, or walk. But please, children and grown-ups, don't ride the buses at all on Monday. Please stay off all buses Monday.

printing three messages per sheet of paper. Working all night, they cut each sheet into thirds and bundled them into stacks for distribution.

At 3:00 a.m., Robinson called E. D. Nixon to let him know what she was doing. Nixon in turn told her that he was calling a meeting of Montgomery's black leaders for that evening.

As dawn broke, Robinson put some 35,000 leaflets into her car and rushed off to teach her eight o'clock class. Afterward, she called her network of Women's Political Council members and asked for their help in distributing the leaflets. She and her students took off in her car along a previously mapped route. At every street corner, she handed a bundle of flyers to waiting women who then distributed them to schools, businesses, barber and beauty shops, factories, and stores. By two o'clock, nearly every black citizen of Montgomery had seen one.

Don't ride the buses to work, to town, to school, or anywhere on Monday.

E. D. Nixon was also up all night. At 5:00 a.m., he began phoning the city's leading black ministers, such as Ralph Abernathy and Martin Luther King, Jr., to rally support for a boycott. Then he had to rush off to his weekend job as porter on the New York–bound train. On the station platform before he left, he gave a quick interview to Joe Abzug, a sympathetic editor at the white-owned newspaper, the *Montgomery Advertiser*. Abzug, he knew, would write a fair, unbiased article about the long-suffering seamstress and the resolve of the black community. Then, having done all he could, Nixon hopped onto the train.

Parks had no idea of the tempest swirling around her. As soon as she woke up on Friday morning she found the scrap of paper her cellmate had given her and called the number scribbled on it. She reached the woman's brother, who promptly got his sister out of jail. Two days later, when Parks passed the woman in the street, she looked so clean and well-dressed that Parks barely recognized her.

Getting the Black Ministers on Board

Next, Rosa called a friend who owned a black taxicab company. Rosa still had to get to work but had resolutely determined that her bus-riding days were over. When she walked into the basement tailoring shop at Montgomery Fair, her boss seemed surprised that she was calm enough to show up to work that day. "Why should going to jail make a nervous wreck out of me?" Parks said lightly. Later on, though, when the store manager came by and refused to talk to her, Parks realized that her activism would probably get her fired.

At lunchtime, Rosa stopped by the law offices of Fred Gray, which she found abuzz with activity. A reporter from the popular black magazine *Jet* asked Rosa some questions and snapped her picture. The rest of the country would soon learn about the humble, dignified seamstress who dared to defy the South's segregation laws.

That Friday evening, Rosa Parks joined a meeting of some seventy black ministers and leaders at Dr. King's Dexter Avenue Church. King, only twenty-six years old, had been minister at Dexter Avenue for little more than a year. He already had plenty on his plate. His wife, Coretta, had recently given birth to their first child and King had just finished his doctoral dissertation. When his friend Ralph Abernathy tried to convince him to help organize the boycott, King had at first protested that he needed to concentrate on his church responsibilities. Yet Abernathy argued that the opportunity could not be lost. Persuaded, King opened the basement of his church for a meeting.

The ministers could not agree on what to do. Should they support the boycott and advertise it in their Sunday sermons? As they debated, Parks stood up to speak. In her dignified way, she explained the daily humiliation of bus travel to these ministers, most of whom owned cars and had no need to use the buses themselves. Persuaded by her and other women, the ministers agreed to support the boycott in their Sunday sermons and then to meet again Monday evening to assess the situation after the one-day

At first, Martin Luther King, Jr., was reluctant to get involved with the boycott. He was a fairly new minister and his first child, Yolanda, had just been born. She is shown here with her father in 1964.

boycott. Parks helped rewrite a shortened version of Robinson's boycott flyer that appeared on the front page of the *Advertiser*. On Sunday, pulpits in black churches across Montgomery rang with support for the boycott.

The Boycott Begins

Rosa Parks held her breath. Would black Montgomery answer the call? Early on that drizzly Monday morning, she peered out her window—and saw an empty bus rumble down Cleveland Avenue. Across town on South Jackson Street, King also waited for evidence of success or failure. He and Coretta had estimated that if even sixty percent of black Montgomery citizens cooperated, the boycott could be judged a success. At 6:00 a.m., he saw the first bus go by empty—and then the second. Elated, he jumped in his car and toured the city—and observed a fleet of empty buses.

All across the city, the sidewalks were crowded with people. Office workers, maids, cooks, and handymen trudged resolutely to work, cheerful yet determined. In black neighborhoods, excited children ran after the buses, shouting, "No riders today!" It soon became evident that the boycott had nearly one hundred percent participation. "Never before had black people demonstrated so clearly how much those city buses depended on their business," Parks remarked later. "More important, never before had the black community of Montgomery united in protest against segregation on the buses."

Montgomery city buses like this one had few or no passengers as their black customers stayed away to support the boycott.

Rosa's Trial

Meanwhile, Rosa and Raymond Parks took a cab to the city hall for her trial. The steps were crowded with well-wishers, more than five hundred of them, who had arrived to support her. They craned their necks to catch sight of Parks in her elegant black long-sleeved dress, gray coat, white gloves, and black velvet hat trimmed with pearls. One of the members of Parks's NAACP Youth Council, a girl named Mary Frances, caught sight of her and called out, "Oh, she's so sweet. They've messed with the wrong one now!" As Parks passed through the courthouse doors, the crowd immediately took up the refrain, "They've messed with the wrong one now!"

It wasn't much of a trial. To support the charge that Parks had violated the state segregation laws, the prosecutor called bus driver James Blake as the primary witness. He was followed on the stand by two white women who lied and said that there had been a vacant seat that Parks refused to take. Parks herself never testified. Within five minutes she was found guilty and ordered to pay a fine of fourteen dollars. Defense lawyer Fred Gray immediately declared that he would appeal the verdict to a higher court. Parks spent the rest of the afternoon in Gray's office, answering the phone and telling people what had happened. Yet she was so modest that she never identified herself by name.

> *As Parks passed through the courthouse doors, the crowd immediately took up the refrain, "They've messed with the wrong one now!"*

A Historic Meeting

The mass meeting that night was held at the huge Holt Street Baptist Church. Everyone knew that the one-day boycott had been successful. Now they had to decide what Montgomery's black community should do next.

By the time Parks arrived at the church, thousands of people had already gathered in the streets outside and in the church itself. Loudspeakers had been set up so that those who could not fit into the church could still hear the proceedings. She had to push her way through the standing-room-only crowd to reach the platform, where a chair had been set aside for her.

The meeting began with a rousing performance of the hymn "Onward, Christian Soldiers." E. D. Nixon then spoke briefly, predicting that the boycott would be "a long, drawn-out affair."

An inspirational Martin Luther King, Jr., addresses the overflow crowd at a mass boycott meeting at the Holt Street Baptist Church.

Earlier that afternoon, the ministers had chosen Reverend King as the president of the new Montgomery Improvement Association (MIA), which was set up to oversee the boycott. Now, the audience applauded and television cameras rolled as King approached the pulpit. He had jotted down an outline for his speech just twenty minutes before. Yet as his eloquent words flowed on, the crowd was thrilled.

King began by praising Rosa Parks. "I'm happy it happened to a person like Rosa Parks," he said, "for nobody can doubt the boundless outreach of her integrity. Nobody can doubt the height of her character; nobody can doubt the depth of her Christian commitment." He spoke of how the black citizens of Montgomery had been abused and mistreated for too long.

He spoke of how the black citizens of Montgomery had been abused and mistreated for too long.

"But there comes a time that people get tired . . . tired of being segregated and humiliated; tired of being kicked about by the brutal feet of oppression. . . . But we have come here tonight to be saved from that patience that makes us patient with anything less than freedom and justice. . . . If you will protest courageously and yet with dignity and Christian love, when the history books are written in future generations the historians will pause and say, 'There lived a great people—a black people—who injected new meaning and dignity into the veins of civilization.' That is our challenge and our overwhelming responsibility."

The church erupted in cheers and applause. They continued standing as Rosa Parks was introduced. "Rosa, Rosa," the crowd chanted.

Finally, the Reverend Ralph Abernathy read aloud a resolution calling for a continued boycott. It stated that black people would stay off the buses until—first, black riders were treated courteously; second, they were seated on a first-come, first-served basis, starting in the back of the bus; and third, black men were the bus drivers on the mostly black routes. The resolution passed unanimously. "This is just the beginning!" someone shouted out.

As Martin Luther King, Jr., wrote in his book about the Montgomery Bus Boycott, *Stride Toward Freedom*, "That night we were starting a movement that would gain national recognition; whose echoes would ring in the ears of people of every nation; a movement that would astound the oppressor, and bring new hope to the oppressed."

The modern civil rights movement had officially begun.

The front page of *The Montgomery Advertiser* for Tuesday, December 6, 1955, shows a picture of the previous night's packed gathering at the Holt Street Baptist Church and the headline "5,000 At Meeting Outline Boycott."

CHAPTER 8

The Walking City

[Rosa Parks] was the heroine. They saw in her courageous person the symbol of their hopes and aspirations.

—Martin Luther King, Jr.

For the next twelve and a half months, black Montgomery walked. Rather than submit to a system they hated, people stayed off the buses and found whatever other means of transportation they could: carpools, taxis, and above all, their own tired feet. Throughout the ordeal, their spirit remained strong and their will unconquerable.

Certainly they were fortunate in the leadership of Martin Luther King, Jr., a brilliant man of enormous persuasive abilities and ingenious resources. "King has captured the imagination and the devotion of the masses of the Negroes here and has united them," Virginia Durr wrote a friend. They also derived inspiration from Rosa Parks, the woman who started it all. To thousands, she became a symbol of resistance, an "angel walking," as one black citizen said.

To thousands, she became a symbol of resistance, an "angel walking," as one black citizen said.

Transportation Troubles

Three days after the mass meeting, on December 8, King and other MIA officials formally presented the boycott demands to city commissioners and bus company representatives. They emphasized that they were not demanding an end to bus segregation, just to unfair treatment. Attorney Fred Gray even pointed out that another segregated city, Mobile, Alabama, already had a first-come, first-served policy on their buses. Yet, no matter what the MIA members said, the commissioners and the bus company refused to budge. Nothing, the commissioners insisted, would change.

As documented in this February 1, 1956, photograph, African Americans took to the streets of the "Walking City" during the 381 days of the bus boycott.

A group of African Americans get into a car as an empty Montgomery bus rumbles by behind them.

Christmas was coming, and the air was getting colder. It was vital that a temporary system of transportation quickly be patched together so that people could continue to get to jobs and stores. Eventually the MIA Transportation Committee organized some 325 private cars to pick up passengers from forty-three stations every morning and another forty-three stations in the evening.

Donations raised from individuals, black businesses, church offerings, and bake sales paid for gas and other expenses. As the boycott was publicized, and donations began to come in from around the country, the MIA bought twelve station wagons. Altogether, the committee enabled 30,000 boycotters to get where they wanted to go.

Black housekeepers, in particular, were the "foot soldiers" in this campaign. Those who could trudged long miles to homes where they might have worked for decades. Many white women were so alarmed at the thought of losing their maids that they gave them rides every day. When Mayor W. A. Gale rebuked them for helping the boycotters, these women wrote letters to the newspaper. One snapped, "If the mayor wants to do my wash and wants to cook for me and clean up after my children let him come and do it. I'm certainly not going to get rid of this wonderful woman I've had for fifteen years."

No one had any idea how long the boycott would go on. Parks recalled that "some people said it couldn't last, but it seemed like those who said that were the white people and not us. The whites did everything they could to stop it." The police threatened to arrest taxi drivers who did not charge the full fare, and bullied carpool drivers and blacks at pick-up stations. Many disgruntled whites fired their black employees. Other blacks were simply unable to get to work.

Out of Work but Not Out of Hope

Rosa Parks was one of those people. On January 7, 1956, she was let go from her job at Montgomery Fair. The store did not admit it was firing her because of the boycott. Rather, the official

Rosa Parks took various sewing jobs after losing her job at Montgomery Fair.

explanation was that the tailor shop itself was closing, and that Rosa's services were no longer needed. She took home two weeks' **severance pay** and some bonus money. The boycott made it impossible for her to get another regular job, and she took in sewing at home to get by.

A week later came an even worse shock. Raymond Parks had worked for years at the barbershop on Maxwell Field Air Force Base. Suddenly his boss declared that any one who discussed "the bus protest or Rosa Parks in his establishment" would be fired, so Raymond quit in protest. How could he work someplace where he couldn't even mention his wife's name? No one else was willing to employ Rosa Parks's husband either, so he stayed home

On January 27, 1956, Martin Luther King, Jr., enthusiastically discusses the boycott with Montgomery Improvement Association leaders, including the Reverend Ralph Abernathy (seated left) and Rosa Parks.

and, unfortunately, started to drink too much. Rosa began to worry about him.

Unemployment was a "blessing in a way" for Rosa, because it gave her time to help out with the boycott. Now, as a member of the MIA Executive Board, she volunteered as a dispatcher for the Transportation Committee, directing cars to pick up passengers. On some days, she worked from 5:50 in the morning till midnight at the old ham radio in the MIA's office.

As the boycott continued, national and international newspapers and magazines publicized what was happening in the "Walking City." Well-wishers from around the country sent clothes and shoes, often addressed to Rosa herself, which she in turn passed out to people in need. New shoes came in especially handy for those who had worn theirs out on the hard sidewalks of Montgomery. For Rosa came gifts from around the world: letters of support from Ghana, telegrams from Paris, prayer beads from India.

The White Community Strikes Back

Bad feelings between blacks and whites in Montgomery continued to worsen. Mayor Gayle still refused to negotiate, and called the MIA "a group of Negro radicals." Martin Luther King, Jr., was arrested for a trivial charge—driving five miles per hour above the speed limit—and then his house was bombed. A day later, when E. D. Nixon's house was bombed, too, Rosa ran over to help clean up. Luckily, in both instances, no one was hurt.

Although their house was never bombed, the Parks family was besieged by threatening phone calls. Voices on the other end would hiss, "You're the cause of all this. You should be killed," Parks recalled. Even worse were the times when her terrified mother or husband would pick up the phone.

Martin Luther King, Jr., calms down an upset black crowd from his porch after his home was bombed on February 4, 1956. With him, from left to right, are Montgomery's fire chief, mayor, and police commissioner.

Working Through the Courts

The MIA did not respond with violence but filed a federal lawsuit challenging bus segregation laws. It stated the laws were "separate but unequal" in keeping with the precedent reached in *Brown v. Board of Education*. Rosa's appeal had already been dismissed by a district court, and this new case was filed on behalf of four other female plaintiffs who had also refused to obey Alabama's bus segregation laws. The MIA hoped to take *Browder v. Gayle*, as the case was called, all the way to the Supreme Court.

In February, the frustrated white community tried another tactic. A grand jury indicted eighty-nine black leaders, including Rosa Parks, for violating an old law that made boycotts illegal. Parks marched herself down to city hall again, where she was photographed being fingerprinted by a young policeman. The

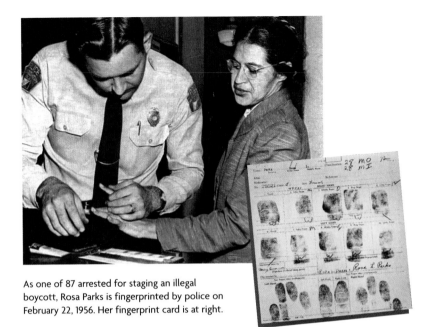

As one of 87 arrested for staging an illegal boycott, Rosa Parks is fingerprinted by police on February 22, 1956. Her fingerprint card is at right.

photograph was published on the front page of the *New York Times* on February 22, 1956.

In the end, the only defendant who actually went to trial was King. He was convicted of disobeying the anti-boycott law and sentenced to pay $500 in fines or spend 386 days in jail. The unjust verdict only made him even more popular in the eyes of African Americans nationwide.

Speaking Out on the Road

Parks had also become famous, and offers of speaking engagements kept pouring in. Like King, Abernathy, and Nixon, she spoke at church rallies and NAACP meetings to raise money for the boycott. At the suggestion of her old friend at the

Martin Luther King, Jr. (1929–1968)

By the time Dr. Martin Luther King, Jr., preached his first sermon at Dexter Avenue Baptist Church in 1954, he was already a man of considerable achievement. He owed his profound religious convictions and pride in his race to his father, who was pastor of the Ebenezer Baptist Church in Atlanta. After earning his undergraduate degree at Morehouse College, he attended divinity school at Crozier Theological Seminary in Pennsylvania and earned his doctorate at Boston University.

Leadership of the Montgomery bus boycott launched him on a career as the foremost American civil rights leader of the twentieth century. In the course of his career, King would give 2,500 speeches, be arrested more than twenty times, and be assaulted four times. In 1964, at age thirty-five, he became the youngest man—and only the second African American—to be awarded the Nobel Peace Prize.

On April 3, 1968, King spoke of his conviction that his dream would be realized at last: "I've been to the mountaintop. . . . And I've looked over. And I've seen the Promised Land. I may not get there with you. But I want you to know tonight, that we as a people will get to the Promised Land." The next day, at age thirty-nine, King was assassinated.

Dr. Martin Luther King, Jr., shown here at a 1964 press conference, emerged as the leader of the civil rights movement between 1955 and 1968.

Eleanor Roosevelt sits with Autherine Lucy, the first black student to attend the University of Alabama. Both women joined Rosa Parks at a civil rights rally at Madison Square Garden, New York in May 1956.

Highlander School, Myles Horton, she traveled north in May to speak at Madison Square Garden in New York City. It was a trip full of firsts—first airplane ride, first visit to New York City, first Chinese food, and her first meeting with former First Lady Eleanor Roosevelt. Mrs. Roosevelt was known for her support of civil rights and friendship with African American leaders. In her newspaper column "My Day," Roosevelt talked about meeting Rosa Parks: "She is a very quiet, gentle person and it is difficult to imagine how she ever could take such a positive and independent stand." It was not the first time someone had misunderstood Parks's deceptively reserved demeanor.

Tired and Exhausted

The next stop was Detroit, Michigan, where in addition to raising money, Parks also visited with her brother Sylvester and his wife and family. Then it was on to San Francisco, California, in June. By this time, Parks was exhausted and ready to go home.

She was unprepared when a belligerent white reporter started asking her nasty questions. "He announced arrogantly that he was going 'to take me apart and see what made me tick,'"

Roy Wilkins was the executive director of the NAACP for 22 years, from 1955 to 1977.

she recalled in her autobiography. "He was trying to intimidate me, and he succeeded." The tea cup in her hand began to shake, and Parks broke down and began crying hysterically. The reporter sneered at her and walked away.

Later Parks recalled that she sat in the hotel lobby crying for a half hour before anyone seemed to notice her. Finally Roy Wilkins, the national head of the NAACP, saw her distress and came over to offer comfort. "It's all right, Rosa," he said, putting an arm around her shoulders. Gradually, she calmed down.

That summer seemed especially long and hot in Montgomery. In June 1956, the federal district court ruled in favor of the MIA in the bus desegregation case. The boycotters couldn't celebrate yet, however. The city commissioners immediately appealed to the Supreme Court and continued to try to break the boycott. The Parks family was deluged by hate mail and phone calls every day. In August, Rosa took a much-needed break, attending a workshop at the Highlander School in Tennessee with a supportive white minister, Robert Graetz, and his family. While they were there, Graetz received the message that his home had been bombed. There seemed no escaping the hate.

Victory at Last

Finally, the long wait came to an end. On November 13, 1956, the U.S. Supreme Court ruled that bus segregation was unconstitutional. It was "a victory for the unity of mankind!" a jubilant King exclaimed. "At bottom, the universe is on the side of justice." He warned the cheering crowds gathered at the Holt Street Baptist Church, though, that no one could get back on the buses until the court released the official written order. They had been patient this long. They would just have to wait a little bit longer.

> *On November 13, 1956, the U.S. Supreme Court ruled that bus segregation was unconstitutional.*

Rosa spent the time back at Highlander School, this time with her mother by her side. She was invited to encourage six black students from Tennessee to continue to try to integrate their local public schools. One boy, for instance, who had been attacked by a few white boys, needed strategies for coping and for leadership development. Myles Horton found Parks so persuasive and effective that he offered her a full-time job at Highlander teaching the principles of nonviolence to teenage groups across the South. Leona McCauley, though, put her foot down. She told Rosa in no uncertain terms that she did not want to live anywhere where she saw "nothing but white folks."

The long-awaited court papers eventually arrived on December 20—and the next day, African Americans got back on the buses. Naturally, the national press was there to record the great moment. King, Abernathy, and Nixon, as Parks wrote, "made a great show of riding the first integrated bus in Montgomery" at 5:45 in the morning. Three reporters from *Look* magazine showed up on Rosa's doorstep and persuaded her to go downtown with them for a photo opportunity.

She got on and off a few buses and then boarded a Cleveland Avenue bus—and was displeased to discover that the bus driver was none other than her old foe James Blake. She sat in one of the front seats, with the reporter behind her, and a photographer snapped a picture of her looking out the window. The resulting photograph became the most famous image ever taken of Rosa Parks.

[Rosa] was displeased to discover that the bus driver was none other than her old foe James Blake.

The Montgomery bus boycott had lasted 381 days. It represented a crucial step in American democracy, promising all a renewed chance to achieve the freedom and equality promised in the Declaration of Independence and the Constitution. By joining forces to take responsibility for their own destinies, ordinary black Montgomery citizens modeled the type of nonviolent protest that would propel the civil rights movement to ultimate success. However, there were rough waters ahead—for the country, for the movement, and for Rosa Parks.

This iconic photo of Rosa Parks riding the newly integrated Cleveland Avenue bus was taken on December 21, 1956. The man sitting behind her was a reporter.

CHAPTER 9

New Directions

It didn't feel like a victory. There still had to be a great deal to do.

A great victory had been won—yet to Rosa, the battle for equality had barely begun. In Montgomery, after two days of calm, the violence started all over again. Snipers were taking pot shots at buses, and someone fired a gun through King's front door. Four black churches and two ministers' homes were bombed. Still, the buses continued to run.

In the Parkses' home, the hate mail kept coming. One phone call was so threatening that Raymond Parks took to sleeping with a loaded gun nearby. Rosa was particularly worried about the effect the threats were having on her husband. He seemed so agitated that Rosa thought he was having a nervous breakdown. Also, there was

In the Parkses' home, the hate mail kept coming.

the effect of the stress on her mother, whose health was never very good. Some evenings, Leona would spend hours on the phone with a friend just to block the vicious phone calls.

In despair, Rosa called her cousin, Thomas Williamson, in Detroit and told him about the threats. Come to Detroit, he said immediately. The racists can't reach you there.

Rosa reluctantly realized she would have to move. It wasn't just the harassment that was bothering her. It was the attitude of her fellow civil rights workers in the Montgomery Improvement Association.

Changes Brought by the Boycott

The Montgomery boycott had changed all of their lives in unexpected ways. It had given Martin Luther King, Jr., a national forum and a goal. After the success of the bus boycott, King wanted to bring the "Montgomery experience" to other southern communities, so in January 1957 he formed the Southern Christian Leadership Conference (SCLC) to carry the torch of desegregation across the South.

For Rosa Parks, the successful boycott had made her a recognizable symbol, and with her fame came invitations to speak at church and NAACP functions across the country. Unfortunately, her status as heroine made some of the male ministers jealous. "Oh, here's the superstar," they would say jokingly when she entered the room. Even E. D. Nixon made disparaging remarks about her, telling someone she was a "lovely, stupid woman." Such remarks hurt Rosa Parks greatly.

In any event, being known as a "troublemaker" meant that

An elegant Rosa Parks attends an NAACP Prayer Pilgrimage for Freedom in May 1957. After the boycott, she continued to participate in NAACP and SCLC events.

Southern Christian Leadership Conference

Following on the heels of the Montgomery Bus Boycott, Martin Luther King, Jr., brought a group of sixty black preachers to Atlanta in January of 1957 to coordinate civil rights protests. They called their new organization the Southern Christian Leadership Conference (SCLC) and named King as its president. Telegrams sent to President Dwight Eisenhower and other government officials declared that the SCLC, dedicated to nonviolent resistance, would enable African Americans to "seek justice and reject all injustice."

Small town organizations sprang up in towns and cities to organize voter registration drives and **sit-ins** at local lunch counters. For the next decade, the SCLC organized protests and marches in many communities, most famously in Albany, Georgia, and in Birmingham and Selma, Alabama. Although it lost some of its influence when Dr. King was assassinated in 1968, the SCLC continues to fight discrimination today.

This SCLC voter registration rally in Selma, Alabama, in March 1965 helped lead to the passage of the federal Voting Rights Act later that year.

Rosa and her husband would never be hired in Montgomery's white community again. "To be a heroine is fine, but it does not pay off," her friend Virginia Durr said about Rosa. For more than a year, Parks had made do with occasional sewing work and the help of friends. Now she needed a job.

In the summer of 1957, she packed up a lifetime's worth of possessions and memories and prepared to move to Detroit.

In the summer of 1957, she packed up a lifetime's worth of possessions and memories and prepared to move to Detroit. Before they left, the MIA gave her a farewell event and gave them a going-away gift of $800. Then it was good-bye, Montgomery.

A New Life in Detroit

After a short stay with Rosa's cousin, the Parkses moved into a small apartment on the West Side of Detroit. Rosa's brother Sylvester had moved to the Motor City—the capital of America's car industry—more than ten years before, and he had a steady job as a mechanic in Chrysler's automobile plant. Raymond Parks

This current photograph shows the skyline of Detroit, Michigan, the city to which the Parks family moved in 1957.

began to attend barbershop school to get his Michigan license while Rosa babysat her thirteen nephews and nieces and looked for a job.

She found one, but it was far away from Detroit. The president of Virginia's Hampton Institute, the famous black college that Booker T. Washington had attended, wanted her to be hostess of its guest house, the Holly Tree Inn. It was an offer Parks did not want to turn down.

It was while she was at Hampton that on September 20, 1958, Parks received a very special parcel in the mail: a signed copy of Martin Luther King, Jr.'s new book about the Montgomery bus boycott, *Stride Toward Freedom*. As she sat down to read it, a bulletin came over the radio: King had been stabbed at a book signing in Harlem in New York City. A crazed woman had run at him with a penknife. Rosa fell to her knees, sobbing and praying that King would not die. Friends who called the hospital in New York on her behalf found out King was in surgery. Soon the word came that King had had two ribs and part of his breastbone removed, but he would survive.

Parks felt relieved, but was very lonely at the Hampton Institute. She was tired of being far away from Detroit and from the most important people in her life. At the end of the year, she went back to Detroit for the holidays, and she did not return. She missed her husband and mother too much.

On September 30, 1958, Coretta Scott King kisses her husband Martin as he recuperates in his hospital room from a stab wound delivered ten days earlier.

Instead, she went to work at a small sewing factory, the Stockton Sewing Company, in downtown Detroit. For five years she sewed women's aprons and skirts on a Singer power-industrial sewing machine, content with a steady, low-stress job so close to home. Her co-workers were friendly, too. One of them, a sixteen-year-old student from a local high school, was thrilled to find out that the kind middle-aged woman sitting next to her was none other than the famous Rosa Parks. Elaine Eason Steele chatted so much with her newfound friend that she was soon fired. Parks had greatly enjoyed the girl's energy and spunk, though, and the two remained in touch.

Attending a small church in her neighborhood, Saint Matthews African Methodist Episcopal (AME) Church also kept Parks occupied. Her religious faith, always a source of strength and solace, sustained Rosa as she served in church functions and helped needy and homeless people. In 1964, Parks accepted the highest honor a layperson could receive—she was made a deaconess (a female church officer) of the church. Week after week, "Sister" Rosa cared for these people and helped during the services of baptism and the Lord's supper.

Moving with the Movement

Of course, Rosa's true passion remained the growing civil rights movement. As an honorary member of King's SCLC, she continued to be invited to speak about the boycott. She often flew back to the South to attend big marches and conventions.

One particularly memorable event was a 1962 SCLC convention in Birmingham, Alabama. Dr. King was just wrapping up his keynote speech when suddenly a white man from the audience jumped onstage and started punching King in the face. To Rosa's astonishment, King dropped his hands and did nothing to protect himself. He was literally "turning the other cheek," as the Bible had told him to. "Don't touch him! We have to pray for him," King ordered his followers.

Confused, the attacker paused. Immediately he was surrounded and led away. Parks left her front-row seat and ran backstage, where she found King holding an icepack to his aching head. She gave him her own remedy for a headache: two aspirins and a Coke. To Parks, the incident was "proof that Dr. King believed so completely in nonviolence that it was even stronger than his instinct to protect himself from attack."

Parks had mixed feelings about nonviolence as a method for changing people's minds. Growing up, she had found it necessary to defend herself verbally from attack—and to make it clear that she was prepared to defend herself physically, as well. "I was raised to be proud," she once wrote, "and it had worked for me to stand up aggressively for myself." She never forgot the image of her grandfather, shotgun across his knees, sitting in his rocking chair and waiting for the Klan.

In principle, she believed that only the threat of violent revenge could guaranty safety. Yet she had witnessed a nonviolent protest work successfully in the bus boycott. She eventually came to the conclusion that "the civil rights movement of the 1950s and 1960s could never have been so successful without Dr. King and his firm belief in nonviolence."

The March on Washington, D.C.

To support a landmark civil rights bill that President John F. Kennedy had introduced to Congress, Martin Luther King and other civil rights leaders organized the March on Washington, D.C., to be held on August 28, 1963. The event drew more than 250,000 people, black and white, to the capital. It was during

Peaceful Protests

Martin Luther King, Jr., adopted the philosophy of nonviolent resistance (also called passive resistance) for the civil rights movement. He was inspired by Mohandas Gandhi, an Indian activist who said that one should resist oppression firmly but peacefully, without any use of violence. In his book, *Stride Toward Freedom*, King outlined the five major points of nonviolent protest:

In February 1960, college students staged a successful sit-in at Woolworth's segregated lunch counter in Greensboro, North Carolina. Soon this form of peaceful protest spread throughout the country.

1. The method "is not passive nonresistance to evil, it is active nonviolent resistance to evil."

2. Nonviolence "does not seek to defeat or humiliate the opponent, but to win his friendship and understanding."

3. "The attack is directed against the forces of evil rather than against persons who happen to be doing the evil."

4. One must be willing to "accept blows from the opponent without striking back."

5. "The nonviolent resister not only refuses to shoot his opponent but he also refuses to hate him. At the center of nonviolence stands the principle of love."

One of the most successful forms of active nonviolent resistance came to be known as sit-ins. Throughout the South, black college students started to sit down at white-only lunch counters. Many of the protestors were arrested—but one by one, the lunch counters were desegregated. All of this happened without protesters ever throwing a punch or firing a shot.

"I Have a Dream"

The most lasting legacy of the 1963 March on Washington would be Dr. Martin Luther King's "I have a dream" speech. He had worked on the speech feverishly the night before, writing and rewriting parts of it. Yet when he came to the podium to address the crowd, he ended up departing from his prepared text halfway through. Instead, he repeated the "I have a dream" theme that he had used many times before in sermons to all-black audiences. This time, before a national television audience, he said to all America, "I have a dream that one day this nation will rise up and live out the true meaning of its creed: "We hold these truths to be self-evident, that all men are created equal. . . . I have a *dream* today!" President Kennedy, watching on a White House TV, turned to an aide and praised the speech. Later, he met King and the other leaders of the march in the Cabinet Room. "I have a dream," echoed Kennedy, shaking King's hand.

President John F. Kennedy poses with organizers of the March on Washington, August 28, 1963.

Showing solidarity, black leaders of the historic March on Washington lock arms together as they walk down Constitution Avenue. Martin Luther King, Jr., can be seen in the center.

this rally that Dr. King gave his legendary "I have a dream" speech in front of the Lincoln Memorial.

Although the turnout was tremendous, Rosa was dismayed to find that no women civil rights workers could march with the male leaders of the rally and that the program in front of the Lincoln Memorial included no female speakers. Instead, there was a "Tribute to Women," in which she, along with workers like Septima Clark, was introduced to the crowd. The only African American women included in the program were singers Mahalia Jackson and Marian Anderson.

"Nowadays, women wouldn't stand for being kept so much in the background," Parks wrote years later, "but back then women's rights hadn't become a popular cause yet." She never forgot the slight against women at the March on Washington. The civil rights movement was radicalizing Parks in unexpected ways.

CHAPTER 10

A Time for Change and Sorrow

It seemed like we were losing everybody we thought was good.

The civil rights movement was at its height in the mid-1960s. Martin Luther King, Jr., continued to challenge segregation across the South with his use of nonviolent strategies. From Oxford, Mississippi, to Birmingham, Alabama, to Nashville, Tennessee, a wave of marches, protests, and sit-ins upset the Jim Crow laws and riveted the attention of the nation.

In November 1963, President Kennedy was assassinated, and the new president, Lyndon B. Johnson, pushed through the Civil Rights Act that Kennedy had introduced to Congress earlier that year. It was also the same Act that the March on Washington had supported in the summer of 1963. On July 2, 1964, in the presence of Dr. Martin Luther King, Jr., and other civil rights leaders, President Johnson signed the Civil Rights Act of 1964.

Working for a Politician

Meanwhile, as black candidates entered politics in sizeable numbers for the first time since Reconstruction, more African Americans began holding local and even national offices.

The Civil Rights Act of 1964

The Civil Rights Act of 1964 was the first major civil rights legislation since the Reconstruction era. After introducing the bill to Congress, President John F. Kennedy explained its necessity to the nation in a televised speech in June 1963: "The Negro baby born in America today regardless of the section of the nation in which he is born, has about one-half as much chance of completing high school as a white baby born in the same place on the same day; one third as much chance of becoming unemployed . . . a life expectancy which is seven years shorter; and the prospects of earning only half as much." By banning racial segregation in public places; outlawing job discrimination on the basis of race, religion, gender, and national origin; and establishing uniform voting standards, the Civil Rights Act attempted to eliminate the legal basis for segregation and discrimination.

Martin Luther King, Jr., looks on triumphantly as President Lyndon B. Johnson signs the 1964 Civil Rights Act on July 2, 1964.

One such candidate was John Conyers, a young lawyer who ran for Congress in Michigan's First Congressional District in 1964. Rosa Parks was active in his campaign, answering phones and doing mailings. Not only did she grant Conyers her personal endorsement, but she persuaded King to make a public endorsement of her candidate as well. After winning the election, a grateful Conyers offered Parks a job as a receptionist and general assistant.

Rosa Parks worked for Congressman John Conyers for more than twenty years. In this 1968 photo, Congressman Conyers (left) is shown with Martin Luther King, Jr.

Parks traded in her sewing machine for a typewriter and on March 1, 1965, began work in Conyers's new Detroit office. There she would stay until September 30, 1988, when she retired at age seventy-five. Over the years she answered mail, organized voter registration, and found jobs and housing for people in need— many of the same functions she had performed years before, for E. D. Nixon at the NAACP. Only this time, she was paid.

Having Mrs. Parks in his office provided Conyers with a double benefit. Not only did he gain an able office assistant, but also "Rosa Parks was so famous that people would come by my office to meet with her, not me," he noted. He was always impressed by her unfailing dignity and polite manner. "It was bizarre," he said. "She never got into an argument, yet controversy was always swirling about her. . . . She had a heavy progressive streak about her that was uncharacteristic for a neat, religious, demure, churchgoing lady."

Another Road to Civil Rights

Rosa Parks could, in fact, be more radical than others in the SCLC. While King was preaching nonviolence, Parks found herself intrigued by a black leader who stood for active resistance against white racism. His name was Malcolm X, the charismatic

Malcolm X (1925–1965)

Malcolm X's troubled and brilliant career made him a hated figure to some, a hero to others. Born Malcolm Little, he grew up poor and desperate in Michigan and Boston, turning early to a life of drugs and petty theft. While in prison on burglary charges, he converted to the Nation of Islam, a religious sect that followed Muslim teachings but also advocated black separation from white America.

After his release in 1952, he cast off his "slave name" and called himself Malcolm X. As spokesman for the Black Muslims, Malcolm became known for his fiery, often anti-white speeches. Yet in 1964, he had a change of heart after making a pilgrimage to Mecca, the holy city of Islam. There, after meeting Muslims of every race and nationality, he began to feel that equality of the races was a possibility. "I realized racism isn't just a black and white problem," he said. "It's brought bloodbaths to about every nation on Earth at one time or another." Conflicts within the Nation of Islam made Malcolm fear for his life, and on February 21, 1965, he was assassinated by members of the Black Muslims.

Nation of Islam leader. Rosa did not approve of his hatred of white people, yet she "had a lot of admiration for him," she admitted, especially his stand against alcohol and drugs and his message that blacks should be strong and stand up for themselves. "Dr. King used to say that black people should receive brutality with love, and I believed this was a goal to work for," Parks said, "but I couldn't reach that point in my mind at all. . . . Malcolm wasn't a supporter of nonviolence, either."

Malcolm X (right) and Martin Luther King, Jr., (left) both fought for civil rights but used different approaches. They met only once, on March 28, 1964, in the halls of the U.S. Capitol.

Confrontation in Selma

Violence seemed to infect all areas of the civil rights movement. One of the most shocking instances was the march from Selma to Montgomery on Sunday, March 7, 1965. It had been organized to protest the disenfranchisement of black citizens in Alabama and the voting rights problems across the South. As six hundred civil rights supporters marched out of Selma onto the Edmund Pettus Bridge, mounted police and Alabama state troopers advanced and began clubbing the marchers and throwing tear gas. Parks was one of millions of horrified Americans who watched the footage of "Bloody

Sunday" on national TV that night. She was also one of the 25,000 people who heeded King's call to come to Alabama and continue the march.

On March 25, Parks flew into Montgomery for the first time in eight years. She joined the other marchers at a campsite outside town, where that night celebrities such as Harry Belafonte; Peter, Paul, and Mary; and Johnny Mathis entertained the crowd. The next morning, she joined the group for the last eight miles to the capitol building.

When Rosa had left Montgomery many years before, she had been one of the most recognizable people in Montgomery. However, by 1965, a whole new generation had come of age in her old hometown, and these young people did not know her. Because she arrived late, Parks was not wearing the right color to signify that she was one of the leaders of the march. Organizers kept pulling her out of the front of the march and pushing her to the sidelines. Then someone would recognize her and say, "Mrs. Parks, come on and get in the march." Back in she would go, only to be pushed out again.

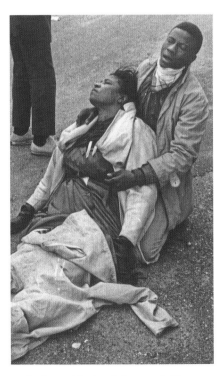

Civil rights activist Amelia Boynton Robinson was gassed, beaten, and rendered unconscious in the violent clash on Bloody Sunday.

Twenty-five thousand people completed the march from Selma to Montgomery on March 26, 1965. The front line of civil rights leaders included the Reverend Ralph Abernathy (third from left), Ambassador Ralph Bunche (fifth from left), and Dr. Martin Luther King, Jr., with his wife, Coretta. Rosa Parks joined the leaders after this photograph was taken.

Finally, as they neared the capitol building, she was pulled back into the front line again. As photographers flashed their cameras, Parks linked arms in a row with Martin Luther and Coretta Scott King, Ralph and Juanita Abernathy, U.S. Diplomat Ralph Bunche, and Roy Wilkins, head of the NAACP. Parks sat on the speakers' platform with the other notables and took the microphone to say a few words about the Highlander Folk School.

Martin Luther King, Jr., the keynote speaker, recalled those days when he and Rosa had led the bus boycott ten years before. He reassured his listeners that they were still "on the move, and no wave of racism will stop us!" Despite its awful start, the march was considered an important success. Tens of thousands of marchers went home marveling at how seemingly peaceful and nonviolent it had all turned out to be.

More Violence and Riots

Rosa remained troubled, however. In her nightmares that night, she dreamed that she and her husband were out in a large field next to a billboard. Suddenly a white man in blue jeans appeared from behind the billboard and pointed a rifle at her. Jolted awake, Parks turned on the news and heard the horrific news of another murder. Violet Liuzzo, a white woman from Detroit who had come to Montgomery to support the march, had been shot and killed by Ku Klux Klansmen on a highway outside the city. The second Selma march had claimed a victim after all.

A shaken Parks attended Liuzzo's funeral in Detroit and threw herself into the cause. At a Women's Political Action Committee dinner (a tribute to Parks) in April 1965, she lamented Liuzzo's death and urged continued action. That August, when President Johnson signed the Voting Rights Act into law, Parks was at the White House to witness the historic occasion.

Violet Liuzzo, murdered after the Selma march, is shown in happier days in Detroit, Michigan, with her children.

The Voting Rights Act of 1965

The march from Selma to Alabama, as its organizers had hoped, did help to pass new national voting rights laws. The day after Bloody Sunday jolted the nation. President Johnson addressed a joint session of Congress to announce that he was placing a new Voting Rights Act before Congress. "Rarely are we met with a challenge . . . to the values and the purposes and the meaning of our beloved Nation," Johnson said. "The issue of equal rights for American Negroes is such an issue. . . . The command of the Constitution is plain. There is no moral issue. It is wrong— deadly wrong—to deny any of your fellow Americans the right to vote in this country." The Voting Rights Act of 1965 outlawed the literacy tests and poll taxes that had long kept African Americans from voting in the South. Within a year, the number of registered black voters in Alabama shot up from 66,000 to 250,000.

Even with the passage of the Voting Rights Act, racial tensions remained high. Over the course of the next few years, riots broke out in forty-three cities across America. One of these was Detroit. Beginning on July 23, 1967, the city erupted in an eight-day violent spree of looting and burning. It took seven thousand U.S. National Guard and Army troops to restore calm. Parks regarded the destruction with disgust. This was not civil rights, she said. It was not black pride. It was vandalism and thievery. Raymond Parks's barbershop was one of the many black-owned businesses looted that week. In the end, 43 people died, 463 were injured, 388 families were left homeless, and the city—with $40 to $80 million worth of property damage—smoldered.

Police search suspected looters during the 1967 Detroit, Michigan, race riots.

The End of an Era

An even greater blow fell on April 4, 1968. Martin Luther King, Jr., in Memphis, Tennessee, to support a garbage-workers strike, was shot and killed on the balcony of his motel. Rosa and her mother were listening to the radio when the news broke, and they prayed and wept together. With her friend Louise Tappes, Parks flew to Memphis to talk to the strikers. She soon realized that the demonstration would not continue due to the death of King. She then accepted singer Harry Belafonte's offer to fly with him in his private plane to King's funeral in Atlanta, Georgia.

At the funeral she met Senator Robert Kennedy, who at the time was running for president in the Democratic primaries.

The nation fell into grief at the death of Martin Luther King, Jr. Mourners at King's gravesite on April 9 included his three children (left), widow Coretta Scott King (center), and singer Harry Belafonte (right).

Shortly afterward, she had a dream about King and Kennedy together. Two months later, Robert Kennedy was also assassinated. It was a decade of deaths—John F. Kennedy, Malcolm X, Martin Luther King, Jr., and Robert F. Kennedy. "It seemed like we were losing everybody we thought was good," Parks thought despairingly.

The dream of equality certainly had not died. In fact, the political and social gains made by African Americans in the 1960s would usher in decades of expanded opportunity and achievement.

CHAPTER 11

Mother of the Civil Rights Movement

What had begun as a simple act of civil disobedience ended up galvanizing the modern movement for civil rights.

——President George W. Bush, December 1, 2005

Rosa Parks returned to Montgomery in 1975 for the twentieth anniversary of the bus boycott. Everywhere she looked she saw evidence that the civil rights movement had made a difference. Although the theme of the anniversary was The Struggle Continues, clearly African Americans had made many social and political gains over the course of the previous two decades.

Alabama, which had had no black lawmakers in 1955, now boasted fifteen in the state house of representatives and senate. In 1968, Shirley Chisholm had become the first black female member of

Shirley Chisholm was not only the first African American woman elected to Congress but also, in 1972, the first African American to run for president.

the U.S. Congress. Black mayors had been elected in many cities; black studies courses had been instituted in colleges; black writers, artists, athletes, and musicians had gained new or even greater national prominence. A proud Parks urged conference members at the Holt Street Baptist Church to "Keep on. Keep on keeping on." In her honor, Cleveland Avenue, the street in Montgomery down which she had taken the by-now famous Cleveland Avenue bus, was renamed Rosa Parks Boulevard in 1965.

Parks's private life, meanwhile, had become more difficult. In the 1970s, her mother, brother, and husband all struggled with cancer. Rosa had to cut back to part-time work at John Conyers's office as she traveled back and forth to three hospitals. Raymond Parks died first, in 1977. His loss was a cruel blow to Rosa, who had depended on his affectionate companionship for forty-five years. Even though, as he got older, Raymond retreated from involvement in the civil rights movement, his private love and support were crucial to Rosa's continued activism.

Sylvester McCauley died just three months later. "Words can't explain the double loss I felt," Rosa recalled years later. "It was a sad, sorrowful, time." Because she had to go back to work, Parks put Leona McCauley in a nursing home and visited her three times a day. Finally, worn out, she moved into an apartment house for senior citizens with her mother. Rosa nursed her until Leona died in 1979 at age ninety-one.

Renewal and Rebuilding

Grieving and in ill health, Rosa faced life alone. Luckily, she still had her job at John Conyers's office and her friends at the Saint Matthews AME Church. She also had Elaine Eason Steele— her co-worker at the Stockton Sewing Company so many years before—who had remained her good friend and essentially became the daughter she never had. Steele took over the management of her affairs, helping her answer her fan mail and traveling with her to conferences and other activities. Steele taught Parks to turn down speaking engagements and interviews when she was tired or ill; Parks was too polite to say no.

Gradually, Parks found a new purpose in life: She had always loved being around young people. In 1987, with the help of Steele, she founded the Rosa and Raymond Parks Institute for Self-Development to "offer programs for youth to help them continue their education and have hope for the future." The highlight of the program was an annual Pathways to Freedom bus trip to historic places in the black experience, especially the Underground Railroad route from Virginia to Canada. Sometimes Parks would go along on the trips, too. "We didn't know if we should clap or bow when we first met her," one student admitted.

In her later years, the honors earned by a lifetime of achievement came flooding in. In 1979, she received the Spingarn

More than three decades after refusing to give up her seat on the bus, Rosa Parks, seen here just before her 75th birthday in 1988, was still working toward a better future for all citizens.

On November 28, 1999, Rosa Parks shows off the Congressional Gold Medal of Honor with Vice President Al Gore at her side.

Medal, the most prestigious award of the NAACP. In 1996, President Bill Clinton awarded her the Presidential Medal of Freedom, the highest U.S. award for nonmilitary citizens, and in 1999 the U.S. Congress gave her the Congressional Gold Medal.

That year, *Time* magazine named her one of the twenty most influential people of the twentieth century. She also received awards, medals, and honorary doctorates from organizations and universities in the United States and around the world. The Rosa Parks Library and Museum in Montgomery opened in December 2000.

When Rosa decided to share her story with the world, she chose writer Jim Haskins as her collaborator on her first book, *Rosa Parks: My Story* (1992). As befitting her lifelong involvement with young people, she aimed her autobiography at a young audience. This book was followed by the inspirational volume *Quiet Strength* (1994) and *Dear Mrs. Parks: A Dialogue with Today's Youth* (1996), a collection of her letters to children.

In her later years, the honors earned by a lifetime of achievement came flooding in.

Despite her nationwide fame, in her old age Rosa Parks still lived a simple, frugal life. On August 30, 1994, the eighty-one-year-old Parks was assaulted by an intruder in her small West Side Detroit apartment. Demanding money, the young black man began to hit and shake her. Parks gave him the $53 in her purse and begged him to go away. He did, but the nation was outraged by this attack on one of its icons. "This is inconceivable," Detroit police chief Isaiah McKinnon fumed. "This lady was responsible for changing the course of this country." Parks ended up moving to a high-rise apartment overlooking the Detroit River. There, in the last years of her life, she gazed out at the ships and barges moving up and down the river, contemplating the past and imagining the future.

President George W. Bush pays his respects to Rosa Parks, whose body lies in state in the U.S. Capitol on October 30, 2005.

A Final Tribute

Rosa Parks died on October 24, 2005, at age ninety-two. Her body lay in state in the U.S. Capitol for two days, making her only the twenty-eighth person—and the first woman—to be given that honor.

On November 2, more than four thousand people attended her funeral. "She didn't just stumble into history," the Reverend Jesse Jackson said at the funeral service. "She was a tough, smart woman who made a judgment to take on the whole system." Former president Bill Clinton said that Parks had started "the most significant social movement in modern American history, to finish the work that spawned the Civil War and redeem the promise of the Thirteenth, Fourteenth, and Fifteenth Amendments."

The Rosa Parks Bus

The most famous bus in history was nearly lost forever. When James Blake's old Cleveland Avenue bus was retired from service in 1971, bus company managers ordered officials of the Montgomery branch to dump it into a river. Memories of the bus boycott were still too fresh and painful, and many thought those days, and Rosa Parks's bus, were best forgotten.

However, two Montgomery employees dared to disobey headquarters, and instead saved the bus by selling it to state patrolman Roy H. Summerford, who wanted some old buses for extra storage space. For thirty years, Bus No. 2857 rusted away in a field in Alabama. Summerford ripped out its seats and sold its engine, while its lime-green-and-yellow exterior faded andchipped. He kept the story of the bus alive, though, and after Summerford's death in 2001, his family sold the bus at auction.

After Rosa Parks died, the restored Cleveland Avenue bus in the Ford Museum in Dearborn, Michigan, was draped in black and purple in her memory.

Those thirty years had also seen an upsurge of public interest in the early civil rights movement and interest in the bus ran high. After a fierce bidding war, the Henry Ford Museum in Detroit snapped up the bus for $427,919. Now restored to mint 1955 condition, Bus No. 2857 is visited every year by thousands of school children. When Rosa Parks died, the bus was draped in purple and black bunting to memorialize the woman who made it famous.

On December 1, 2005, buses around the country honored Rosa Parks by keeping one seat empty. This poster on a New York City, bus reminds passengers that "It All Started on a Bus."

On November 2, she was buried in a Detroit cemetery. The headstone reads:

ROSA L. PARKS
1913–2005
MOTHER OF THE MODERN DAY
CIVIL RIGHTS MOVEMENT

On December 1, 2005, exactly fifty years after Rosa Parks refused to give up her seat on the bus, President George W. Bush signed a bill ordering that a statue of Parks be erected in the U.S. Capitol's National Statuary Hall—right next to the statue of Confederate president Jefferson Davis. "What had begun as a simple act of **civil disobedience** ended up galvanizing the modern movement for civil rights," Bush declared.

That day, dozens of bus systems around the country, including in New York City; San Francisco, California; and Boston, Massachusetts, honored Parks in a unique tribute, by keeping the seat behind the driver empty. In New York, a taped poster on the seat read, "It All Started on a Bus."

Glossary

abolitionist—a person who wants to abolish, or get rid of, slavery.

anti-Semitic—showing prejudice or bias against people of the Jewish faith.

apartheid—official South African policy of racial discrimination against nonwhites until the 1990s.

boycott—the refusal to buy or use certain goods or services.

civil disobedience—nonviolent protest against social injustice.

class action—a lawsuit in which one or more individuals represents the interests of a whole group.

disenfranchise—to take away the right to vote.

Great Depression—the period of economic hardship in America from 1929 to 1941.

integration—bringing together people of different ethnic or racial groups on a basis of equality.

lynched—put to death, usually by hanging, without due process of law.

minstrel show—a popular nineteenth-century variety show featuring white performers in "blackface" makeup.

plaintiff—a person who brings suit in a court case.

precedent—a person or thing that serves as a model; especially in a court of law.

radicals—people who hold extreme political views.

Reconstruction—the period after the U.S. Civil War when Congress passed laws expanding the rights of freed slaves.

segregation—the separation of people of different races, classes, or ethnic groups.

severance pay—the money paid to employees after they have lost their job.

sharecropper—a farmer who rents a piece of land from an owner using a portion of his crops grown on the land.

sit-ins—nonviolent demonstrations in which people sit down and refuse to move.

Supreme Court—the highest court of the United States.

Uncle Tom—a derogatory term for a black person who is subservient to white authority, from a character in Harriet Beecher Stowe's novel *Uncle Tom's Cabin.*

white supremacists—people who feel the white race is superior and show extreme prejudice toward other races, especially African Americans.

World War I (1914–1918)—the war fought between the Central Powers (Germany, Austria-Hungary, Bulgaria, and the Ottoman Empire) and the Allies, especially Great Britain, France, Italy, Russia, and the United States.

World War II (1939–1945)—the war fought between the Allies (Great Britain, France, the Soviet Union, the United States, et. al) and the Axis powers (Germany, Japan, and Italy).

Bibliography

Books

Branch, Taylor. *Parting the Waters: America in the King Years, 1954–63*. New York: Simon & Schuster, 1988.

Brinkley, Douglas. *Rosa Parks*. New York: Viking, 2000.

Crawford, Vicki L., Jacqueline Anne Rouse, and Barbara Woods, eds. *Women in the Civil Rights Movement: Trailblazers and Torchbearers, 1941–1965*. Brooklyn, New York: Carlson, 1990.

Garrow, David, ed. *The Walking City: The Montgomery Bus Boycott, 1955–1956*. Brooklyn, New York: Carlson, 1989.

King, Martin Luther, Jr. *Stride Toward Freedom*. New York: Scribner, 2001.

Olson, Lynne. *Freedom's Daughters. The Unsung Heroines of the Civil Rights Movement from 1830 to 1970*. New York: Scribner, 2001.

Parks, Rosa. *My Story*. With Jim Haskins. New York: Dial Books, 1992.

Robinson, Jo Ann. *The Montgomery Bus Boycott and the Women Who Started It*. Knoxville: University of Tennessee Press, 1989.

Washington, Booker T. *Up from Slavery*. New York: Doubleday, 1901.

Williams, Juan. *Eyes on the Prize: America's Civil Rights Years, 1954–1965*. New York: Viking Penguin, 1987.

Web Sites

The King Center
www.the kingcenter.org

The Martin Luther King Jr. Research and Education Institute
www.stanford.edu/group/king/

The National Civil Rights Museum
www.civilrightsmuseum.org

The Rosa Parks Bus at the Henry Ford Museum
www.hfmgv.org/exhibits/rosaparks/default.org

Rosa Parks Library and Museum at Troy University in Montgomery
Montgomery.troy.edu/rosaparks/museum

Rosa and Raymond Parks Institute for Self-Development
www.rosaparks.org

The National Civil Rights museum
www.civilrightsmuseum.org

Image Credits

About the Author

Ruth Ashby has written many award-winning biographies and nonfiction books for children, including *Herstory* (Viking), *Pteranodon: The Life Story of a Pterosaur* (Abrams), and *The Amazing Dr. Franklin* (Peachtree). She lives on Long Island, New York with her husband, daughter, and dog, Nubby.